# SECURITY
# AND PRIVACY
# IN AN
# IT WORLD

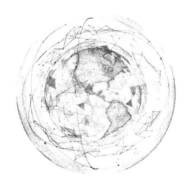

# SECURITY AND PRIVACY IN AN IT WORLD

Managing and Meeting Online Regulatory
Compliance in the 21st Century

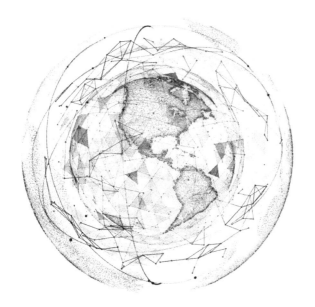

# CRAIG MACKINDER

Published in 2017 by
Kinetics Design, KDbooks
kdbooks.ca,
linkedin.com/in/kdbooks

ISBN 978-1-988360-14-0 (paperback)
ISBN 978-1-988360-15-7 (ePUB)
ISBN 978-1-988360-16-4 (ePDF)

Note for librarians: Canadian Cataloguing in Publication Data
for this book is available from Library and Archives Canada
at www.collectionscanada.ca/amicus/index-e.html.

Edited by Michael Carroll, mrpcarroll1@gmail.com

Book design: Daniel Crack, Kinetics Design,
kdbooks.ca, linkedin.com/in/kdbooks

*This book is dedicated to my children.
I hope they will look back at this book and laugh
a little at how far technology has advanced from
the time of its writing to their adulthood.*

# Contents

# Introduction

THE EUROPEAN UNION has a digital privacy act, as does Canada, the United States, and countries around the world. Every day it seems nations are enacting new laws meant to protect their citizens and their government networks from other nations.

In a world ever more dependent on technology to function, protectionism and cybersecurity fears threaten global commerce. So how is cybersecurity managed while also respecting privacy laws and meeting the many new and emerging regulations governing data collection domestically and abroad?

First, this book will examine the root cause of this insecurity around the world. What has led to a reversal of the free and open Internet for e-commerce even among European partners? Will laws such as the European Union Data Protection Directive (EUDPD), Personal Information Protection and Electronic Documents Act (PIPEDA), and Federal Information Security Modernization Act (FISMA) end up hurting the free flow of business online?

Second, this book will take a look at the effectiveness of these laws in their attempt to thwart, hinder, or prevent cyberattacks. Could it be that these disparate and sometimes conflicting laws are creating more vulnerabilities than a unified global regulatory strategy could achieve?

Finally, and most important, this book will discuss what these regulatory changes mean for business information technology (IT). Some businesses are hiring IT regulatory experts in-house as part of their legal team, while others are turning to third-party providers to ensure they are in compliance. Which strategy works best and should compliance issues be left to a chief information officer (CIO)?

Every company is different, and business goals will dictate what kind of investments need to be made to meet compliance obligations. The goal is that by the end of this book the reader will know how best to navigate the changing regulatory landscape and have a much better understanding of its legal implications.

# 1

# The Business Cost of Internet Freedom

*The Internet is the first thing that humanity has built that humanity doesn't understand, the largest experiment in anarchy that we have ever had.*

— ERIC SCHMIDT, EXECUTIVE CHAIRMAN OF ALPHABET, INC.[1]

## Monday Morning in Japan

It was uncommon to have a cell phone back in 1999. It was even more uncommon when my cell phone rang at 11:00 p.m. on a Sunday night. But as the systems administrator in a growing manufacturing company, I knew what the ringing meant.

It was the director of information technology calling. His monotone instructions came through the tiny speaker: "Grab your keys. I need you to meet me at the office. I haven't been able to access the accounting systems for the past two hours."

After arriving at the office and checking only a handful of computers, I found something similar in every system. The Happy99 e-mail virus had penetrated and infected several computers, and those computers were shutting down the limited capacity of our network.

"Okay, well, let's turn off the Internet and everyone will just have to *stop* using e-mail!" shouted the director in his most sarcastic tone. We knew very well that shutting off the Internet and e-mail might have been acceptable a decade earlier. But in 1999 at this American subsidiary of a Japanese manufacturing behemoth the Internet and e-mail systems were the lifeblood of the entire operation.

Although the company manufactured heavy equipment, everything outside of the assembly floor — accounting, sales, customer service, human resources, and executive management — required Internet connectivity and communications. Keeping these systems running was mission-critical, and it was the reason we were standing in the office at one in the morning!

It took several hours, but finally we removed the last remnants of the infection and blocked the incoming infected e-mails. Our security policies had failed to block this new threat, but our security response procedures gave us a clear and effective path to recovery.

Our co-workers started their Monday morning without interruption. The main office in Japan could send over sales leads, work orders, and invoices and continue normal business operations … while the other world governments allowed it.

Today, in the scenario above, it might not be as "simple" as removing a virus from a foreign subsidiary's network. Regulatory hurdles might be preventing doing the job.

There might not be access to important network data because of data localization. In fact, it might even be the host country that sent the attack. A growing sense of protectionism across the globe is now threatening the free and open commerce the Internet has enabled.

All advanced nations are coming up with new regulatory strategies for protecting their own IT networks and forcing all other nations to comply. How can IT professionals and business decision-makers prevent these new measures from making global e-commerce too costly? Can the Internet stay free, or will the costs of protectionism be too great?

## Examining the Biggest Threats to Global E-Commerce

Free trade, globalism, and e-commerce all have something in common: they are intricately and perhaps indivisibly tied to the Internet. It is what helped make the Internet free and open for all these years. However, this level of Internet freedom is now being challenged by protectionism on multiple fronts:

- Global and domestic Internet security.
- Intellectual property rights.
- Individual privacy rights.
- National sovereignty.
- Business expansion.
- International trade.
- The concept of freedom itself.

At the heart of these challenges are underlying insecurities. China feels threatened by U.S. dominance in cyberspace, so now its leaders have begun instituting protectionist measures to tip the playing field in their favor, particularly against U.S. technology firms. Russia, as well as other nations such as Iran, Turkey, and Pakistan, is mostly unnerved by America's technological military capabilities. U.S. citizens are feeling threatened by cyber criminals and hackers who are constantly finding new ways to disrupt, damage, and destroy their cyber lives. And businesses in general are always afraid their innovations and business growth will be stifled by onerous regulations that end up causing more problems than they solve. Meanwhile, all of this is happening against a background of a virtually lawless digital landscape that is constantly being shaped by a confluence of geopolitics, business interests, and consumer demands.

## Trade Made Global E-Commerce Possible

Politics is inextricably tied to the Internet because it was trade policy surrounding Internet technology that made the current global economy possible. Furthermore, corporate interest is also inherently tied to the Internet, and it was business interests that helped push policies to open up commerce through a free and open Internet.

At the forefront of this push were American business and government leaders. Seeing the practically immediate benefits of this new technology, the United States realized that the productivity gains and wealth creation brought about by the Internet would only increase with broader access resulting in a rapid expansion of Internet accessibility through the late 1990s and first decade of the 21st century.

Building on the decades-old infrastructure created during the previous technological boom in radio and transportation technology, new inroads were laid that facilitated global e-commerce. Markets where business investment was once fruitless suddenly became viable with new opportunities for business expansion.

Along with those changes came calls from a few corners to slow down the pace of technological revolution, but those calls were drowned out by the voices of business, governments, and individual consumers. Quite the contrary, the United States and other industrialized nations that were reaping huge rewards from these changes helped press for global trade agreements that encouraged more Internet expansion and more global e-commerce.[2]

Not everyone came out a winner during this expansion. Some nations were locked out of this economic boon. For example, the former Soviet Union came late to the revolution as did many other developing and Third World nations. While those nations have tried to make up for lost ground during the past several years, the United States has continued to push the envelope for what is possible in a globally connected world.

Wealthy countries such as the United States where the world's leading tech firms reside continue to separate from the pack, creating an uneven playing field. This disparity between the tech capabilities of the United States and those of, say, Brazil is part of what is fueling a rise in protectionism that threatens to make global e-commerce too costly. Even as nearly half the world's population is connected to the World Wide Web, more people in fewer than two dozen countries have been left out of this expansion.

## Global E-Commerce Requires Broad Internet Access

According to a study conducted in 2016, an estimated four billion citizens around the world don't have access to the Internet.[3] Of those people, 90 percent live in developing nations that are already decades behind the rest of the world in Internet technology.

Since by some estimates, just connecting more people to the Internet increases a nation's total GDP, places lacking access and that need it the most experience an ever-widening gap with connected countries. In the United States, Internet access has resulted in GDP growth of about 3.5 percent. In Europe the productivity gains have been even bigger, seeing a nearly 20 percent increase in productivity as a result of e-commerce.[4]

The more access a country has the faster it can process information, payments, shipments, and more. Because anyone can start and build a business totally online, small and midsized businesses begin to thrive where individuals and businesses have unfettered access to the Internet. Mom-and-pop shops can compete on a global scale thanks to the type of Internet freedom to which advanced nations have become accustomed.

As a result, commerce itself has completely changed. It is only because of the Internet that tech firms can sell products without investing in manufacturing physical objects. Software programs that previously had to be shipped on CDs and installed on the user end can now be paid for, downloaded, and installed in minutes, sometimes seconds.

Big data is now aggregated quickly and easily so that sales information, consumer statistics, and logistic strategies can be altered based on real-time information to improve business operations, marketing, and profitability. Nowadays, information and big data are sometimes even more valuable than real investment dollars to a business because of the results that can be achieved.

However, that data is at the heart of a lot of the recoiling occurring around the world. There is a level of trust that goes with global e-commerce. When users download services and pay for them, they want to make sure their data is protected. When foreign consumers log on to a website — that is if their government allows it — how much of their personal data will the business collect?

Mix in the growth of the mobile Internet and the IoT (Internet of Things) and now there is so much data circling the globe containing enough information about the business or its individual consumers to be absolutely frightening. Individuals were the first to begin questioning the lack of privacy controls on the Internet.

Governments have long instituted policies to protect their networks, and now businesses are starting to question how much data collection is really necessary. How does cross-data flow affect national sovereignty? In China where the "Great Firewall" monitors and censors the Internet, how can business be done with that country's citizens if data can't be stored on servers back in the United States?

## Six Main Factors Contributing to Protectionism

Inevitably, when so many competing interests vie for the same space, there will be conflict. At that moment conflict manifests itself in protectionist laws that make data security a priority for each nation by claiming sovereignty over consumer and government data. In fact, current trade agreements developed to deal with data security in a globalized world all contain some measure designed to limit cross-border data flow.

At the same time individuals and governments around the globe have become dependent on cross-border data flow to process transactions in real time regardless of location. This interdependence is what makes the trending protectionism happening around the world so disconcerting: what happens to global e-commerce if customers can't be reached outside a nation's borders?

So why are so many nations willing to sacrifice the obvious economic benefits of a globalized economy in the name of security? Aren't there ways to overcome the security issues driving protectionism short of shutting down whole sectors of the global population from the global economy? To answer these questions, it helps to take a closer look at the main factors contributing to protectionism. Here are the top six:

## 1. Global and Domestic Internet Security

On the Internet security front, the problem is multifaceted; it is both a domestic and international problem and is an individual concern for all citizens of the world. Trying to disentangle or brilliantly entangle these interests while maintaining the stability and security of the World Wide Web is at the heart of the problem.

Is it possible to protect online data while also providing a free global space where users have a reasonable expectation their communications are secure from hackers, spying, and data theft? When does cyber policing go too far, and is it worth the risk of a cyber police state run amok?

### Individual Security

First, on the individual level, Internet security and the reasonable expectation of it is imperative for the free flow of e-commerce. Online consumers expect businesses and government agencies to provide a level of security that very few have been able to supply. Even the toughest networks to crack have been exposed by professional hackers, both nation-state actors and lone wolves.

Individuals are targets on multiple fronts. Whether trying to break into personal computers and business mobile phones, or siphoning off data from government files, hackers invade people's private as well public lives, contributing to the creation of protectionist laws and regulations around the world.

### National Security

Recent moves to restrict the flow of data into and out of countries are due in large part to national security fears that were amped up after the Edward Snowden leak of National Security Agency (NSA) files that exposed secret spying both domestically and abroad. The leak included evidence that the United States had been spying on heads of state, even of allied nations, which caused many of them to consider instituting more restrictive Internet security laws.

Businesses all over the world started proposing better security against U.S. spying. A German company, for instance, created its own national version of the cloud, which claimed to be "free from U.S. government surveillance."[5]

Moreover, in more authoritarian governments, many of these new restrictions are passed in the name of national security but are solely a way to control and manipulate their citizens. These governments use Internet data to spy on individuals within and outside their borders.

As long as global Internet security remains disjointed and incoherent, the bigger the landscape for bad actors in the cyber arena becomes. With the expansion of the IoT, mobile, and cloud technology continuing to outpace the means and the rules of the road to secure them, devising coherent global strategies becomes ever more complex.

## 2. Intellectual Property Rights

There is no bigger opponent for the United States than China when it comes to intellectual property rights. As a nation, China, more than any other country, has tried to counter U.S. dominance in Internet and computer technology through intellectual property (IP) theft as well as protectionist measures.

A vast amount of intellectual property in the form of technologies and patents resides within the United States through American companies such as Apple, Google, IBM, Microsoft, Facebook, Amazon, and Hewlett-Packard, to name only some of the more prominent ones. Such a reality breeds insecurity in competitor nations like China — nations bent on reining in U.S. dominance of cyberspace.

Not only is IP theft a big problem but also the fairness of IP rights surrounding technology is a growing point of contention. Advanced nations with an interest in protecting their IP rights want stronger copyright regulations for online content. However, free-speech activists point out that tight copyright regulations help to limit Internet freedom by censoring free speech.[6]

## 3. Individual Privacy Rights

Americans expect and have a legal right to a certain level of individual privacy. Chinese citizens don't. Neither do many citizens around the globe with whom free nations, including the United States, conduct global commerce. If a U.S. business can't assure its consumers that their personal data will be protected, they will lose customers.

At the same time nations such as Canada with which the United States has historically had excellent relations have been cited by Americans for discrimination because of their country's privacy laws.[7] Restricting businesses outside Canada from accessing or storing personal data belonging to Canadian citizens is seen as a trade barrier that impedes global e-commerce.

Other offenders, according to the United States, are the "right to be forgotten" law[8] of the European Union (EU) as well as inconsistent laws from Japan, India, and Chile that present obvious challenges to global norms regarding e-commerce. The Trans-Pacific Partnership (TPP) trade agreement and other new free-trade agreements being enacted are attempting to address these concerns, although the TPP is currently being reassessed by the remaining 11 countries involved in it due to the withdrawal of the United States in early 2017.

However, as with previous efforts concerning global rules of the road governing the Internet, different nations and cultures have different values when it comes to individual privacy. This has led to numerous conflicting and incoherent laws that individual businesses have to deal with from country to country both internally and externally.

## 4. National Sovereignty

Now more than ever national sovereignty is the impetus for many of these new regulations governing the Internet and global e-commerce. Why is the European Union working toward restrictive data-location measures? Like many individual nations, the European Union claims "national" sovereignty as a means to protect its citizens' data from unnecessary collection and storage, but how does a government body know what is necessary and unnecessary?

National sovereignty is also used as a means to limit access for citizens and foreign visitors in order to prevent security risks to business and government networks. On top of that, nations such as China employ national sovereignty as a way to restrict competition against its growing tech industry. Even nations with limited Internet technology are implementing laws to protect them from more technologically advanced nations.

At the root of this reaction is the global insecurity created by the disparity in technological capabilities and Internet access around the globe. Take for instance the growing use of mobile as a primary means for accessing the Internet. In the United States, it is predicted that in just two years nearly 95 percent of Americans will own a smartphone. Compare that to less than 55 percent in the developing world.[9]

## 5. Business Expansion

Businesses naturally only see the opportunities for increasing profits from Internet freedom. When those priorities conflict with government priorities that seek to protect or control their own citizens, regulators typically win the battle resulting in more restrictions, less Internet freedom, and more costly global e-commerce.

Tie that conflict to the many businesses around the globe competing for the same consumer base and it becomes apparent how business expansion touches on all six factors contributing to the current protectionist inclination in the world. Businesses both need their governments' protection while also seeing their governments as the primary thorn in their collective sides.

Intellectual property rights as well as individual privacy rights all intersect with the ability of businesses to function in a global economy. As businesses expand, the need for network security increases, and so, too, do laws using national sovereignty as a means to tilt the playing field against foreign competitors.

## 6. International Trade

Finally, and perhaps most important, is the effect international trade has on global e-commerce and how it contributes to protectionism. There are many products and services that are intangible. Think of web protection services, music downloads, access to information, and more. This is part of what makes coming up with global regulations that work so difficult.

How can data localization requirements as a cloud provider be complied with when servers are maintained in the United States? Previous trade agreements offer little guidance because up until now global commerce almost always involved a tangible product, good, or service to be packaged and shipped abroad. Today much of that is done completely online.

Current moves to restrict data in order to exert national sovereignty and to protect networks from spying and theft could prove costly in the long run. And unlike in the past, network managers have no choice but to be keenly aware of trade policy and how it affects IT compliance.

## Trade Agreements Matter to Network Managers

As nations continue to institute laws protecting their sovereignty, security, privacy, et cetera, trade agreements become ever more important to network managers, whether they are managing their IT networks domestically or abroad. One of the most recent international trade agreements attempting to answer these protectionist measures is the TPP.

During his first week in office, President Donald Trump withdrew the United States from the TPP, which at that time hadn't yet been approved by Congress. With so much political history behind the development of the TPP, it is very likely that another bill encompassing many of the same initiatives previously included in it will be formulated for approval by Congress.

This agreement, while controversial, attempts to use commonsense trade law to govern trade between the United States and its Asian partners, including as it relates to Internet technology and e-commerce. Because of that, in order for network managers to stay in compliance, a closer look at the TPP agreement is necessary.

# 2

# Breaking Down the Trans-Pacific Partnership (TPP)

*As policymakers, we need to foster an environment that allows U.S.-based innovators and entrepreneurs to compete and to flourish. Excessive regulations and bureaucratic red tape dramatically increase the cost of doing business and create uncertainty for companies.*

— U.S. CONGRESSMAN RALPH HALL[1]

*NAFTA and GATT have about as much to do with free trade as the PATRIOT Act has to do with liberty.*

— MICHAEL BADNARIK, 2004 LIBERTARIAN PARTY PRESIDENTIAL CANDIDATE[2]

*The establishment of free-trade agreements can be a critical and progressive step towards greater economic integration, and continues to become more valuable in an increasingly global world.*

— U.S. CONGRESSMAN DAN KILDEE[3]

THE ABOVE EPIGRAPHS TYPIFY THE PROBLEM with navigating the complex regulatory environment the global economy has created. Everyone knows that too much regulation can hinder entrepreneurship and innovation. Everyone knows that some free-trade agreements might have been free but not fair. And everyone knows that without sound rules of the road what is supposed to be a good thing for world economies can become a total catastrophe resulting in the collapse of e-commerce.

No one on either side of the debate wants that. In 2016 President Barack Obama led the way on a new trade agreement between the United States and members of the Pacific bloc that is intended to reduce onerous regulations, improve Internet freedom, and provide rules of the road for governing global e-commerce.

What ensued was a loud and heated debate that pitted those who were all in on the TPP against human-rights groups and unions that argued this trade agreement would actually hurt real people. Ultimately, the surprise victory in the 2016 U.S. presidential election by Donald Trump signaled the TPP's eventual demise in the United States.

At this point it is difficult to surmise any rhyme or reason to Trump's policy edicts. Suffice to say there has been a 180-degree swing from President Obama's full support and leadership on an international trade agreement to the wholly unorthodox approach to trade and regulation exhibited by the new Trump administration — a general zero tolerance for regulations of any kind. Meanwhile, new regulations are popping up around the world that will have a big impact on companies doing business abroad and in the United States, regulations that every CIO and network manager will need to know.

For those who manage IT networks for retail stores' websites where customers can save their credit card information for future purchases, protectionist laws that prevent or hinder cross-border data flow by requiring data to be stored locally can hurt their businesses. The TPP attempted to restrict nations from unduly influencing global trade and e-commerce through protectionist measures.

Since the TPP was the "first of its kind"[4] to attempt to broadly deal with the conflicts that keep nations from making uniform global Internet policy, it is worth taking a closer look at it despite it being seemingly dead in the water in the United States. In the TPP, there are rules of the road that restrict host nations from giving local competitors an unfair advantage in the marketplace. But there are also limits to the power of the TPP to restrict censorship and surveillance.

Cloud providers often service companies from many different industries around the globe, all of which would be affected in one way or another by an enacted TPP. Going forward, the factors that drive the need for a global trade partnership focused on Internet policies still exist. While the TPP didn't purport to fix all of the problems inherent in a loosely regulated global Internet, it would have been an important first step and can still have implications for any future agreements similar to it. Recently, the 11 countries still involved in the TPP announced their desire to continue discussions concerning a revised agreement without the United States, even possibly expanding its membership.

## Pros and Cons of the TPP, but an Important First Step

There are things that both sides can still agree on about the TPP. For one, it was actually the first time a multilateral trade agreement included rules that restrict protectionism relating to the Internet and global e-commerce. Other pros are:

- Updating copyright protections.
- Commitments to facilitate cross-border data flow.
- Rules to keep the Internet open.
- Avenues for legally contesting censorship and network shutdowns.
- New transparency requirements and dispute processes.

All of these issues are items that businesses and governments alike agree hinder a free and open global Internet where e-commerce can thrive. Yet it is important not to be too hasty. Many trade agreements have begun with the best intentions but ended up hurting a lot of people in the end.

More agreement on measures that help all economies prosper is a good thing. However, to make these commitments binding, some things were sacrificed, including limits on the TPP's ability to assist citizens in member nations where free speech online is restricted. There was also little agreement on rules and limits on cybersecurity. The fact is, both sides have strong points and all of them are worth considering.

## What the Critics Have Said

> The Trans-Pacific Partnership is a massive proposed trade deal that would encompass 12 Pacific Rim nations, including the U.S., and 40 percent of the global economy. U.S. presidential nominees Hillary Clinton, Donald Trump and Dr. Jill Stein have all said they oppose the TPP. The deal has faced years of public protest by those who say it benefits corporations at the expense of health and environmental regulations.
>
> — AMY GOODMAN, DIRECTOR OF PUBLIC CITIZEN'S GLOBAL TRADE WATCH[5]

It is easy to get trapped in the tunnel vision of U.S. perspective when thinking about global Internet policy. In fact, that was one of the criticisms launched from other member nations signing on to the TPP. They argued that as far as copyright regulations were concerned, the TPP would have benefited U.S. corporations that already had an advantage over every other country when it came to Internet technology, including intellectual property rights and copyrights.

Proposals for enforcing new copyright regulations contained within the TPP included criminal charges with jail time and enormous fines. Forbidding the sharing of business or government information deemed protected by copyright, TPP critics argued, could prevent whistle-blowers from accessing the information needed to prove wrongdoing, equating to a form of censorship and suppression.

Equally disconcerting for critics of the TPP was the idea that governments or even business competitors in some countries could cry copyright infringement and force a website seizure without any notice or argument from the originator of the content. At the same time, some of the TPP countries that criticized the fact that the United States had the most to gain from the agreement were motivated by self-interest in contesting rules on dispute resolutions for individual privacy infringements.

Oversight provisions in the TPP that would have required more transparency when countries forced network shutdowns were also a point of contention. Even critics who weren't from authoritarian regimes argued that this approach would undermine the rights of sovereign nations to determine their own legal rules for network shutdowns.

Free-speech advocates contended the TPP framers were more interested in protecting corporate rights than they were in defending individual rights. These advocates were backed by big names in global e-commerce, including Google, Walmart, and eBay, to name a few.[6] Their business models, like many consumer-driven global businesses, depend on unfettered e-commerce that requires their support for their consumers' rights relating to Internet access.

## What the Advocates Have Said

> On the merits, it is smart for America to do it. And I have yet to hear a persuasive argument from the left or the right as to why we wouldn't want to create a trade framework that raises labor standards, raises environmental standards, protects intellectual property, levels the playing field for U.S. businesses, brings down tariffs. It is indisputable that it would create a better deal for us than the status quo.
>
> — FORMER PRESIDENT BARACK OBAMA[7]

The last sentence in the above epigraph is the main objection to the TPP from many nations outside the United States, although that objection is countered by the world's reliance on a global trade infrastructure that has in large part been built by U.S. policy. Besides, close allies of the United States and democratic nations around the globe would have benefited from the same measures that helped Americans, though a TPP with the United States did ensure a continuation of U.S. dominance in global trade and Internet policy.

On the copyright issue, where critics argued these rules would have prevented the sharing of important information whether it had public relevance or not, advocates of the agreement pointed to the many exceptions in the new copyright regulations. Specifically, that the guiding principle for what constitutes copyright and public domain is "fair use," which includes sharing:

- Critical commentary.
- News reports citing other sources.
- Learning environments.
- Government and private nonprofit research.

In other words, concerning the TPP, as long as money wasn't earned off the shared copyrighted content, criminal charges weren't applicable. Furthermore, certain governments would have been prevented from blacking out large regional chunks of the Internet to form Internet blocks in which there was no free flow of commerce or ideas.

## The Need for a TPP-Like Agreement on Internet Technology

More than a decade ago what would become the TPP was initiated when several previously closed-off economies agreed in the World Trade Organization (WTO) to lessen their restrictions on trade, including e-commerce. Then, in 2008, the United States joined this effort along with other advanced nations to create a global framework to guide Internet governance for current and future technology. Over time the Internet has changed, business has changed, and the cybersecurity landscape has changed dramatically. If the TPP and its many provisions for Internet technology had gone forward, it would have been applied to a quarter of all global Internet users, greatly influencing the future of global e-commerce.[8]

As will be seen in the next few chapters, the TPP also clashed with some national measures around the globe that are already taking effect, leading to more confusion and disorganization. Now that the deal is dead for the United

States and indefinitely stalled for the other 11 member nations, it is easier to look at parts of the TPP that related directly to Internet technology and governance with clearer eyes, which will help to better inform any future agreements.

### The TPP on Privacy

Just signing up for a newsletter with a name and e-mail address leaves bits of identifying information behind, including cookies that are stored on websites that are visited, along with the Internet provider address. When purchases are made, often the amount of data shared and stored is enough to develop a comprehensive picture of a completely unknown individual, including:

- Name.
- Address.
- Occupation.
- Phone number.
- Credit card information.
- Bank account information.
- Date of birth.
- Driver's license.
- Insurance policy numbers.

Imagine everything that can be gleaned from such information. It is why free-speech advocates are opposed to what they deem to be inadequate measures to address this type of information stored in many business transactions. How long can that information be stored? Is it safer if data storage is restricted by location? How much data is necessary to collect for business purposes? Who is responsible for data breaches that result in financial harm to individuals?

Even businesses that don't deal in retail but harness consumer or business data for analysis will be affected by any new regulations concerning privacy. The TPP's position on privacy was:

- Privacy laws shouldn't be mandated but rather encouraged.
- There should be more transparency and oversight over consumer privacy.
- Enforcement of privacy regulations should be left to domestic courts.
- Health data should be kept locally to comply with stronger privacy laws.
- Signatories will put forth an effort to avoid discrimination in their privacy laws.

- Parties agree to work with other nations to respect their privacy requirements.

Australia, New Zealand, and Canada were among the countries that called for stricter privacy mandates than the TPP ultimately included. However, current law (or lack thereof) provides no oversight or redress for privacy violations in many countries. Australia, particularly, insisted on language that would allow a nation to institute data restrictions without calling it a trade barrier if it can be justified.

On the other hand, any new privacy regulations are an improvement in nations where there have been no such protections. Where global e-commerce is now bringing new wealth to less open nations like South Korea, Taiwan, Indonesia, and Malaysia, such countries are now more willing than ever to respect individual privacy rights in order to enjoy the global economic benefits of the Internet.

Any new countries that refused to sign on to the TPP would have had to adopt these new privacy protections in order to trade with TPP nations. Many advocates argued that would have had its own benefits for privacy law. Yet conceding on the health data localization issue would have created more contention around data localization and the free flow of information for global commerce.

### The TPP on Data Localization

Probably the worst protectionist measure for business is data localization. If all IT firms had to build data centers or offices in every country, city, and state they operate in, it would destroy the clear money-saving advantages of global e-commerce. After the leaks of NSA data revealing U.S. spying on allies, even reliable partners such as the European Union, Canada, and the United Kingdom have instituted protectionist data localization laws that restrict the free flow of cross-border data in business transactions.

In working out their differences while drafting the TPP, the participating nations agreed that protectionist data localization restrictions would have had too harsh an effect on global commerce and trade and therefore relented on previous positions. In fact, they even agreed to language that no TPP nation would institute regulations that would unduly restrict cross-border data and the free flow of information. On data localization and protectionism, the TPP would have:

- Allowed certain exemptions to permit nations to restrict data flow if deemed necessary.
- Restricted the use of data localization to filter out certain websites for censorship or competitive advantage.
- Prohibited data laws that dictated servers must be locally housed and maintained.
- Committed each nation to allow cross-border data flow for the purpose of conducting business.
- Barred spam from the protections afforded to other forms of cross-border data flow.

One of the biggest problems with this part of the TPP was that rules that freed businesses from onerous data localization restrictions didn't pertain to individuals. In fact, the rules specifically only applied to service providers, investments, and/or investors. Human-rights advocates argued that this would have left the door open for oppressive governments to restrict data flows that weren't part of ordinary business as a means to oppress its citizens.

Furthermore, there was no mention of banning spyware or malware that could harm both businesses and governments. Again, though there are many downsides to the TPP, the current lawless state of cyberspace is untenable.

### The TPP on Censorship

For all of the arguments against the TPP, when it comes to censorship, this agreement at least began bringing the Pacific trade bloc more into alignment with global norms against censorship. A Harvard University study done in 2015 and published by the university the following year surveyed more than 7,000 individuals around Asia, asking citizens about their views on Internet freedom.[9]

What was found in the Harvard study is that in the 11 countries surveyed more than 70 percent of their citizens said more protection of free speech online was needed. Fearing their governments, a quarter of them hid their identities online.[10] The nations in the study were Hong Kong, India, Japan, Indonesia, Malaysia, Singapore, Taiwan, Vietnam, Thailand, Pakistan, and South Korea.

Nicknamed the Great Firewall, China's brand of Internet censorship is infamous. The Chinese government has complete control over the country's Internet and uses the Great Firewall to weed out websites and limit the amount of Internet access its citizens can have.[11] This creeping authoritarianism causes huge problems for global commerce, so much so that tech giants such as Google and IBM have had to go dark in China rather than comply with government censorship.

Principled stands against censorship are important enough, but the Great Firewall has also been shown to cost businesses money, making global e-commerce less efficient and more time-consuming. Nearly 80 percent of U.S. businesses argue that China's restrictive censorship laws hurt their operations and bottom lines.

Nations such as Turkey and Syria shut down Internet access whenever they desire, sometimes merely to keep their citizens from capturing government crimes and atrocities on their cell phones and posting them online. Some countries use their government-operated networks to monitor and spy on their citizens. Such nations' principles are in direct conflict with those of the main drafters of the TPP as well as with those of the European Union.

For that reason many believed the TPP fell quite short of the ultimate goal, while advocates argued it was at the very least a start. Despite the many areas of contention, there was agreement on one issue: parties to the TPP had the right to contest or challenge what they deemed to be censorship laws that discriminated against their businesses.

Part of the problem is the difference in values between nations. Another part has to do with sovereignty and no nation wanting to relinquish the power to decide what it deems necessary or unnecessary to protect (or control) its population. Even this one rule in the TPP that all members agreed to faced resistance from some countries considering signing on to the TPP before Donald Trump was elected president.

### The TPP on Transparency

Undemocratic nations that had intended to sign on to the TPP would have seen the biggest changes in how they devised policies governing the Internet in their countries. One of the main requirements aimed at increasing transparency had to do with how Internet policies were enacted. The TPP required governments to publish any new laws or regulations relating to Internet policy for a period of time in order to allow public comment; mandated that all TPP participants had to establish a means to provide oversight for new laws, and parties had to justify such changes to those the measure would affect; and required any new proposal to be supported by sound evidence.

Why would nations that don't believe in democracy sign on to such an agreement? The power of global commerce on their economies is a strong enough motivator to attract support from traditional opponents of such measures. It is yet to be seen how reliably these nations can be counted on to uphold their end of the bargain.

### The TPP on E-Commerce

Information technology providers and network administrators would have been greatly affected by the TPP as it related to e-commerce. Specifically, the job of IT providers is to keep business flowing across borders where protectionist and privacy laws tend to conflict with business objectives. Much of the consternation from opponents of the TPP was concerned with its heavy focus on business interests as opposed to humanitarian and democratic aims.

In the TPP, businesses were covered as service suppliers and services. For example, cloud providers were considered service suppliers because they weren't delivering anything tangible to their consumers. All of their commerce is conducted online. Amazon, on the other hand, would have been classified as a service. Someone in Hong Kong orders a pair of chinos online, which are then shipped from a U.S. distribution center and physically delivered to the destination in Hong Kong.

Because of that, whatever rules applied to a business would have also affected its consumers as well as its long-range plans for expansion into these territories. Some nations wanted those same protections applied to individual users. Although the TPP clause on e-commerce was binding, it allowed for dispute resolution if a company felt that its operations were being unfairly hindered by laws that restricted e-commerce.

### The TPP on Fair Competition

The North American Free Trade Agreement (NAFTA) and many previous free-trade agreements have been roundly criticized today because, though free, many could argue that some of these agreements were anything but fair. The TPP tried to compensate for that by creating rules that promoted not just free trade but fair trade and competition.

Particularly for the contentious relationship between the United States and China over intellectual property disputes and accusations of IP theft, the TPP attempted to prevent any nation from giving its local businesses an unfair advantage. The TPP restricted nations from favoring one provider of digital products and services over another and allowed nations to back their own national firms by supplying them with funding through taxes, subsidization, and grants.

Although it didn't include binding language, the TPP did state that governments signing on to the agreement shouldn't influence or hinder their citizens' rights to choose whichever digital product from whatever company they picked whether it was a local company or one from another country.

While the TPP included provisions that were binding and regulations that were enforceable, any nation could have ultimately reneged on its obligations if it believed its interest to protect the public good and to protect national security were at stake. For opponents of the TPP, this language left the door too wide open for nefarious governments to exaggerate security needs or to apply moral standards as a way to censor or discriminate against other nations.

### The TPP on Cybersecurity

The elephant in the room, finally, was the largely unbinding and vague rules governing cybersecurity that were included in the TPP. The biggest problem the TPP had was that these measures were largely voluntary with no real way to enforce them besides sanctions. Moreover, as stated earlier, there was language banning spam, there was even language addressing data theft, but malware and spyware were largely untouched.

Perhaps the fact that nations such as the United States have begun using malware as a military weapon is why there is little in the way of consensus on cybersecurity. What the TPP did say was that smartphone manufacturers such as Apple had a right, even when national security was invoked by governments, to refuse access to their source codes in order to break data encryption.

On one hand, U.S. companies were happy that the right to refuse access to source codes was included in the TPP. On the other hand, as the IoT expands and smartphones continue to become the primary means for users to get on the Internet, the same firms that have opposed government access to their source codes might want more government protection from mobile malware in the near future.

# 3

# New Regulations Governing Global Internet Business

## The Dreaded SOX 404 Update

The project manager stood up and prepared his position at the front of the room. After two hours of listening to department managers present slides about their areas in desktop support, network engineering, and applications development, it was his turn to update the room of 150 IT department staff. His first slide, "SOX 404 Update," brought an audible sigh from deep in the crowd.

"I know, I know," he said. "This isn't the first time and probably not the last time I'll bring you news about our SOX 404 progress." He was referring to Sarbanes-Oxley Act compliance, also known as "SOX," at a publicly traded company with nearly 2,000 employees. After several months, get-a-handle-on-it fatigue was starting to set in for the entire company.

The chief financial officer (CFO) stood up and interrupted the presentation before the first slide. "Is all of this really necessary? I mean, we want to make sure we're compliant, but do you really need to make a career out of this? When can we say it's done and move on? I need a date."

The vice president of IT came to the presenter's defense. "Next month is the last month for this project. So this will be the last presentation."

The presenter looked stunned and then, in a moment of self-awareness, he quickly hid his reaction. He was shocked at that moment because he knew what we all learn in IT management: while compliance frequently has a start date it rarely has an end date. New laws and guidelines require regulatory compliance to be an ongoing commitment to process improvement, change management, and compliance testing for any business.

Chances are at some point in your work life over the past decade or more you have sat through a few meetings with the company IT department.

Whether it was when you were hired and had to go over Internet policy with your company CIO, or you and other upper-level executives have had to sit through briefings about new system updates.

When IT initiates a meeting, the response above has been typical in many corporate offices. Many IT professionals will even concede the fact that unless someone is in IT, these meetings can be mind-numbingly boring at times. It might even appear that IT guys and gals are "trying to make a career" out of a new update just to boost their own importance.

For CIOs who are constantly butting up against disinterest and apathy when relating important information to company decision-makers as well as to employees, it is utterly frustrating. IT administrators are charged with making sure that company e-mails are free from bugs and functioning properly, satellite employees can access company servers, and traveling personnel have the latest protections on their company smartphones and tablets. The need for all employees to be part of compliance is crucial.

In fact, it is only now becoming more important that leaders of companies begin to get a better understanding of what these regulations mean for everyday operations. If a company is out of compliance, it can have disastrous effects on the business as a whole. Figuring out who should be in charge of compliance isn't always that simple anymore, either. More and more the lines are blurring between what is a function for the legal department and what is IT's responsibility.

In actuality it is a little of both. The businesses of the future will be prepared for any and all new regulations coming down the pike because they have the IT expertise necessary to navigate the winding road of Internet governance. Whether in-house or outsourced, successful IT management requires constant awareness and compliance with ever-changing global and domestic regulations.

## Dealing with Complex and Conflicting Internet Regulations

As complex as the TPP is with its hundreds of pages of legalese, it is just one of the many new regulations and laws coming online governing the Internet for businesses around the globe. Most businesses are working from laws that were passed at least a few years ago. In 2016 alone dozens of countries adopted new rules for business activity online:

- European Union Data Protection Directive (EUDPD) in Europe.[1]
- Personal Information Protection and Electronic Documents Act (PIPEDA) in Canada.[2]

- General Data Protection Regulation (GDPR) update and/or the EUDPD in the United Kingdom.[3]
- Federal Information Security Modernization Act (FISMA) in the United States.[4]
- Golden Shield Project/Great Firewall in China.[5]

Will laws such as the EUDPD, PIPEDA, and FISMA end up hurting the free flow of commerce online? Can the benefits of global e-commerce still be realized with so many conflicting and complicated rules and regulations in place? First, it is necessary to understand what laws governing the Internet are currently on the books. Then, by looking at the legal precedents that created existing law, better ways for constructing new regulations that "do no harm" become more apparent.

This is important because in the digital landscape of today, it is no longer good enough to be well versed in new regulations. Businesses now must be prepared to deal with future laws that don't even exist yet for technology that is only in its infancy or else pay the price.

## Existing Laws

What regulations are intended to do and what they actually do are often two very different things. Generally speaking, when it comes to data protection, for example, there are several identifiable goals for regulators:

- To institute rules and controls that govern how individuals, corporations, and governments interact online.
- To oversee compliance with said rules and controls.
- To develop procedures for enforcing rules.
- To measure compliance.[6]

When it comes to regulating the Internet both domestically and internationally, the rules and controls are murky. Compliance is difficult and often unverifiable, and without clear rules there is no means to enforce regulations, which has led to sometimes ham-handed restrictions that follow old guidelines and protocols that aren't sufficient to deal with new technology.

Take, for instance, one of the oldest laws governing digital copyright in the United States. The law itself is almost 20 years old and is the reason why some websites have "content has been removed" for videos that violate copyrights. The law is called the Digital Millennium Copyright Act and was created to protect websites from suits arising from copyright infringement as a result of user content. Website owners must remove content deemed to infringe on copyrights without facing any legal recourse as an online intermediary.

More to the point, research conducted in 2015 reveals that in countries where there are fair rules governing copyrighted online material, revenue is higher and innovators and creators of new content are able to flourish. In fact, according to one study, the U.S. economy generates close to $5 trillion each year because of its fair use copyright laws.[7] That is in stark contrast to countries where protectionist copyright measures are too restrictive.

What these laws do is remove the fear of liability for website hosts and service providers so that the Internet and the free flow of information can continue. Where there are clear violations of copyright laws, most countries already have laws in place for seeking restitution. But when it comes to digital products and Internet services and service providers, the question of liability looms large over all talks of copyright laws governing digital trade.

## U.S. Laws

The United States has already begun instituting new protections in international trade agreements that spell out rules governing the liability of intermediaries. Today most countries don't have laws in place protecting intermediaries from liability. As the United States continues to strengthen and update international treaties, including the TPP, with more explicit language governing the Internet, these protections will spread to other countries that currently have no such safeguards.

Below are some of the U.S. laws that govern the Internet both domestically and abroad. While some of these laws might seem totally unrelated to Internet technology, that merely demonstrates how complex Internet regulations can be and how practically all laws will be underpinned by rules governing the Internet going forward.

### U.S. Free-Trade Agreements Governing Digital Trade

Currently, there are several free-trade agreements (FTAs) that deal with digital commerce between the United States and other nations. However, there are far more long-standing FTAs that are either outdated or just now catching up to the technology of the past decade. With IT speeding up so rapidly, there is a need to continually update regulations to accommodate the evolving nature of technology, which in turn affects all global e-commerce.

The Trans-Pacific Partnership, as discussed in the last chapter, was the most recent and far-reaching of its kind to attempt to deal with digital trade regulations. This trade agreement had it gone forward would have affected more than a third of the world's trade and commerce.

Antecedent to the TPP is the United States–Korea Free Trade Agreement (KORUS FTA), first drafted in 2007 and finalized officially on March 15, 2012.[8] In it the United States and South Korea have agreed to several regulations on digital trade:

- Extended open-comment periods for new regulations affecting trade.
- Increased protections for intellectual property owners.
- Longer terms for copyrights.
- More enforcement power over copyright, patent, and trademark infringement.
- Greater access to South Korean markets for U.S. service providers.
- Limits on cross-border data restrictions for financial transactions.
- Fewer exceptions for restricting cross-border data flow for businesses.
- Permissions for U.S. investments in and ownership of telecom and broadcast companies.
- Tariff and customs free digital trade.
- Protections for intermediaries against liability.
- Level playing field for foreign trade versus domestic trade.[9]

Since the enactment of the KORUS FTA, U.S. service providers have seen an increase of nearly 35 percent in revenue from exports to South Korea, rising from about $17 billion in 2011 to over $22 billion in 2015, a bigger increase than with any other U.S. trading partner. In addition to further limiting cross-border data restrictions, the TPP would have gone a step farther than the KORUS FTA to prohibit protectionist data localization laws.

Over the past four years that the KORUS FTA has been in effect nearly all industrial products and 80 percent of consumer products are duty free for U.S. companies, while South Korea has seen unprecedented increases in gross domestic product (GDP) and wealth generation. Over the next decade, this trade agreement is expected to bring in a minimum of $10 billion annually due to the cuts on tariffs for exports to South Korea alone.

| U.S. Exports to South Korea | | |
|---|---|---|
| U.S. Exports | 2011 | 2014 |
| Intellectual Property | $4.5 billion | $6.1 billion |
| Travel Services | $5.9 billion | $7.6 billion |
| Professional and Management Services | $697 million | $1.05 billion |
| | | Source: Office of the United States Trade Representative |

### Sarbanes-Oxley (SOX) Act

Thanks to the Enron scandal of the late 1990s, all publicly traded U.S. companies are subject to the Sarbanes-Oxley Act, commonly referred to as SOX.[10] The "dreaded SOX 404 update" and several others back in the 1990s and early 2000s were necessary because of the new reporting mandates included in the 2002 anti-fraud law. Now that nearly all commerce involves gathering and storing financial data online that must be reported, new rules restricting data use and storage means there will be new rounds of SOX updates to comply with international and national privacy laws.

For network managers and IT professionals, section 404 of the SOX Act contains most of the language governing internal controls that affect end-of-year reporting of financials. Overseeing compliance is the Public Company Accounting Oversight Board (PCAOB).

Although it isn't a government agency, the PCAOB was created with a mandate to provide impartial oversight as a nonprofit organization charged with ensuring that all publicly traded company audits are in order. Assessments relating to IT controls include:

- User data management.
- Company audits.
- Financial reporting.
- Data security measures.
- User privacy analysis.
- Access authorizations.
- Authentication requirements.
- Network system development.
- Architecture and network infrastructure management.
- Systems monitoring.
- Backup and disaster recovery protocols.

At the heart of the legislation is the goal to prevent fraudulent record-keeping, which would seem largely to be an accounting issue. However, because most financial reports and the data accrued through that reporting are done so electronically and online, IT managers must be an integral part of *ongoing* SOX compliance.

### Gramm-Leach-Bliley Act (GLBA)

When it was first enacted back in 1999, the Gramm-Leach-Bliley Act (GLBA), which is officially named the Financial Services Modernization Act, was aimed at banks and other financial institutions, not necessarily Internet technology. Yet as financial institutions began securing customer information through the Internet, the requirements of the GLBA have become fundamentally related to information technology. The GLBA requirements include:

- Rules for securing individual personally identifiable information (PII) necessary for financial transactions.
- Annual statement requirements mandating privacy disclosures to consumers.
- Mandates for implementing secure information protocols for financial institutions.
- Testing standards for security measures and practices.

All of the government agencies responsible for regulating financial reporting rely on recommendations from the top five regulatory agencies in charge of financial reporting to assess the need for audits. This group is called the Federal Financial Institutions Examination Council (FFIEC). Since PII, privacy disclosures, and security protocols are all part of any financial institutions business network, IT managers have to be able to ensure these systems are in compliance.

### Health Insurance Portability and Accountability Act (HIPAA)

As we will see later, information protections for health care are at the core of many new European laws that restrict the use and storage of individual health information. The same is true in the United States. Put into force two decades ago, the Health Insurance Portability and Accountability Act (HIPAA) is fundamentally tied to the way many businesses operate in a globally connected world. Whether a company works in the health-care industry or not, simply having employees and providing them with health care means that a company has to comply with HIPAA standards.

For IT professionals, the privacy rules mandated in the HIPAA must also be cross-referenced with international laws governing those same rules for people in other countries. To remain compliant, a business must maintain a network and internal computing system that:

- **Protects Individual Health Information:** The law now includes new regulations for protected health information (PHI) gathered electronically in the administration of health care — termed ePHI. Among other date, it mandates protections for:
  - Medical records.
  - Insurance information.
  - Employment status.
  - Address.
  - Birth date.
  - Credit/bank account information.
  - Social security number.

- **Conceals Identifiable Information of Medical Transactions:** Employers are responsible for having an employer identification number (EIN) when processing or reporting medical transactions to conceal identifiable information.

- **Follows National Coding and Reporting Standards:** The HIPAA standardizes how medical treatments, billings, and PII are kept and reported electronically based on standardized medical codes and identifiers. That includes employers that act as intermediaries between policy holders and insurers through human resource departments and any employee health coverage benefits.

- **Reports Privacy Rules and Changes in Detail:** Businesses must disclose any changes in their privacy rules to all relevant individuals while also providing detailed descriptions of their standard privacy practices.

- **Secures PHI from Unauthorized Access:** The HIPAA mandates any holder of PHI to address security issues by instituting rules to prevent security breaches, unauthorized access to PHI, and sabotage, modification, or deletion of patient records and files.

- **Penalizes Violations of HIPAA Law:** Any violations of the HIPAA can result in criminal charges and costly fines. The HIPAA outlines rules for reporting and investigating HIPAA violations through legal channels.

When the HIPAA was first enacted, few businesses had the infrastructure to support the type of electronic reporting that nearly all businesses do now.

Today businesses can pay serious consequences both domestically and abroad for violating patient or employee PHI privacy laws.

### Bank Secrecy Act (BSA)

Compared to the other laws on the books governing information technology, the Bank Secrecy Act (BSA) is the most antiquated. Passed back in 1970, the BSA was enacted to prevent money laundering. Since then the law has been amended several times and updated. As with many laws that have had to be updated to accommodate modern technology, the BSA affects network administrators because of information storage, use, and privacy requirements:

- **Reporting Suspicious Transactions:** Suspicious transactions, including both deposits and withdrawals of $10,000 or more in cash, or money orders, traveler's checks, or cashier's checks worth $3,000 or more, made in one day must be reported to the authorities by financial institutions authorizing such transactions.
- **Maintaining Secrecy:** Any financial institutions reporting suspicious transactions are forbidden from informing the persons or entities under suspicion that their transactions have been reported.
- **Disclosing PII to the IRS:** Financial institutions are required to report any relevant PII to the Internal Revenue Service (IRS) via a currency transaction report (CTR) if a suspicious transaction is discovered. Even attempting to prevent or get around such accounting must be reported as suspicious activity by financial institutions to the Financial Crimes Enforcement Network (FINCEN) by submitting a suspicious activity report (SAR).

Violators of the BSA face severe penalties if suspicious activity goes unreported. If a company or individual fails to file an SAR or CTR when a dubious deposit or withdrawal has been made or if an actor as part of the financial institution alerts the suspicious actor of a report being filed, the company is held in violation and executives can face felony charges. A lot of modern suspicious activity happens online, and network managers must have the tools and means to monitor that activity on behalf of the company.

### USA PATRIOT Act

After the September 11 attacks in 2001, the PATRIOT Act was enacted to expand federal authority for law-enforcement agencies. The main provision governing Internet systems is the power to pursue suspected terrorists through money-laundering activity. The act gives government agencies permission to violate what had previously been privacy standards contained within the BSA that protects individual PII from undue disclosures. The BSA is only one of several laws that were given an exemption on disclosure if law enforcement deems the information necessary, for instance, to trace money launderers and terrorists through large financial transactions.

### Federal Information Security Modernization Act (FISMA)

The Federal Information Security Modernization Act (FISMA) was put into force in 2002 and was then called the Federal Information Security Management Act. It was largely designed to retroactively beef up the government's IT networks and security systems to combat potential threats by:

- Building up network security throughout the federal government and its contractors.
- Ensuring government information is secure through annual audits.
- Limiting user access to sensitive government information.
- Instituting security protocols that protect:
  – User access.
  – Provide guidelines for security controls.
  – System and network vulnerabilities.
  – Manage PII of government agency and affiliate employees.
  – Secure data collected for official purposes.
- Creating mechanisms for monitoring and enforcing compliance.

Back in 2002 and 2003, government networks were deemed severely deficient with an average score below 70 percent. Recent measurements show improvement compared to international standards. In fact, the World Economic Forum ranks the United States at the top of global nations in cybersecurity with a score of 82 percent in 2016. Yet within the United States small agencies are still woefully underprepared and frequently noncompliant with FISMA, leaving both government and individual information at risk.[11]

According to the Office of Management and Budget (OMB), there were more than 77,000 attempts in 2015 to hack into federal agency networks, with several agencies exhibiting serious vulnerabilities.[12] Still, the report also revealed that more than 80 percent of agencies have ramped up compliance, instituting two-factor authentication (2FA) protocols, and that all 24 agencies were shown to be in compliance with the Chief Financial Officers (CFOs) Act, a part of FISMA governing corporate fiscal decision-makers' obligations under the law.

### Other IT Regulations

The laws above are federal and govern most businesses operating within the United States in one way or another. Specific to IT professionals are the ISO/IEC 27000 standards of the International Organization for Standardization (ISO),[13] a series of guidelines accepted by IT professionals to ensure good practices concerning:

- Information security management.
- Security controls, ethical standards, and codes of conduct.
- Implementation best-practices guidelines.
- Network management security protocols.

It doesn't matter what the industry is — these guidelines ensure best practices for network managers when protecting user data internationally. There are more than 160 countries bound by ISO rules, making them a necessity for network managers to understand as part of their overall business network strategy.

In addition to federal laws, there are state-to-state laws that govern how businesses keep and protect user and business data. California, for example, has an anti-identity theft law that requires businesses to alert their customers whenever they experience a security breach that puts customer PII at risk. This disclosure requirement alone can have big repercussions for a business if its customers begin to lose faith in the ability of the company to protect sensitive information.

Where this requirement isn't mandated, businesses can keep repeated breaches private, leaving consumers at risk to hackers seeking to steal their identities. Many states have begun or intend to institute similar measures to protect their residents. Network managers overseeing national business networks have to be aware of both federal and state laws related to information security now that it is largely done online.

The Federal Trade Commission (FTC) is responsible for enforcing privacy protections covered by federal law. The Civil Rights Office (CRO) is responsible for monitoring compliance with the HIPAA as part of Health and Human Services (HHS). Penalties range from several thousand dollars to potentially millions of dollars. Some violations can result in federal prison time; others might incur harsh sanctions that mandate detailed reporting requirements and supervision lasting decades to ensure continued compliance.

### The Cost of Regulation Violations

Large security breaches have immediate effects on businesses. Consumers are less likely to return to online companies that experience high-profile security breaches. On top of that, if a business is found to be in violation of data protection regulations, it can be sued individually or collectively in a class-action suit. One of the largest data breaches of its kind against a corporation happened in 2013 when Target was attacked on Black Friday.

Hackers gained access to credit card and bank account information for more than 40 million Target customers, and another 70 million had other PII stolen such as addresses, birth dates, and phone numbers. Target had to defend a lawsuit from both its customers and shareholders following the breach. Furthermore, the top executives of the company were brought before the U.S. Congress to testify about the breach, and the firm was investigated by the Attorney General's Office. On average a typical data breach costs businesses in the United States close to $4 million.

### European Laws

Europe offers a particular challenge, further enlarged by Britain's vote in June 2016 to exit the European Union. While the full ramifications of that development are still unfolding, it is a fair assumption that many of the business ties between Britain and the European Union will remain.

Therefore, instead of identifying the IT laws governing business interactions with each of the more than two dozen countries in the European Union, a better guide is the most recent and overarching document governing business interactions using information technology within EU member states — the European Union Data Protection Directive (EUDPD).

#### European Union Data Protection Directive (EUDPD)

Prior to 2016, the European Union Data Protection Directive (EUDPD) governed all data transfers and protections for the members of the European Union. However, in June 2016 Britain put leaving the European Union up for a vote, and surprisingly, the country as a whole voted yes while Scotland and Northern Ireland voted no. For now, the United Kingdom will be considered separate from those states operating under the EUDPD.

Known as the "Directive," the EUDPD has governed Internet privacy and data transfer for European citizens since the beginning of the 21st century. It has been updated over the years to reflect changing technologies, providing the citizens of the European Union with stronger privacy protections than even U.S. law provides. The Directive restricts how long and how much information can be collected that could identify EU citizens and limits the type of data that can be sent outside the European Union to locations that don't meet the EUDPD's standards.

Recently, the Directive has butted up against other international and member state privacy laws, creating the need for a newly revamped and updated data protection measure. Hence, on May 24, 2016, the European Union passed the General Data Protection Regulation (GDPR), which is to go into effect by May 2018. In the meantime, EU states are required to adhere to EUPDR standards.

### General Data Protection Regulation (GDPR)

Like the EUDPD, the General Data Protection Regulation (GDPR) forbids storing or sending PII to countries without adequate user data protection laws that are in line with EU standards. While there are many similarities between the old law and the new updated directive, there are important differences, since the GDPR fundamentally increases privacy protections, putting the onus for compliance on companies within and outside the European Union.[15] Some of the new standards included in the GDPR are:

- A requirement to provide detailed explanations why certain data collection is necessary.
- New disclosure requirements to alert employees of any PII collection and the purpose for it — also requiring consent for data collection.
- Rules for allowing employees to contest or remove permissions for collecting PII at anytime as well as the right to request documentation detailing how that information has been used.
- Ability for users, employees, and customers to request deletion of personal information or correction of incorrect or incomplete personal information online.
- Required development of security protocols for protecting sensitive information, including disaster recovery and response plans.
- Institution of policies to ensure better vetting of third parties, vendors, and contractors.
- Inclusion of whistle-blower protections for reporting violations of the GDPR.
- New accountability measures that make handlers of employee, customer, and end-user data, including network administrators and data processors, liable for mishandling of PII.

In addition to these measures, the GDPR creates several new positions responsible for oversight to ensure compliance with the law. Businesses will need to employ a data protection officer and a data processor by 2018. The law also mandates protocols for designing data protection procedures and requires annual assessments on the efficacy of each company's data protection protocols.

One of the major reasons for this new iteration of EU data protection laws is to unify privacy protections among all EU member states. This is aimed at providing consistent rules and regulations for countries outside the European Union when conducting business. It is important for businesses to understand their obligations under the GDPR before it is enacted. There are stiff penalties for violators, including fines reaching into tens of millions of euros.[16]

## International Laws

As mentioned before, Britain's exit from the European Union, or Brexit, creates a bit of uncertainty in international law. Legally, the United Kingdom will no longer be bound by the GDPR or EUDPD. At the same time, to maintain the long-standing relationships the United Kingdom has nurtured over the past decade and a half as part of the European Union, the country will likely continue to follow the same standards detailed in EU directives. Still, that could change if Britain decides to alter its laws in ways that conflict with EU standards.

For American companies and other nations doing business with the United Kingdom, it will be important to watch what Britain does. There are a few options that could change the relationships between the United Kingdom and its international trading partners.[17] Britain could decide to create a new alignment with the European Economic Area or petition the European Commission to evaluate U.K. data protections to deem the exiting country fit to trade with EU members.

### Personal Information Protection and Electronic Documents Act (PIPEDA)

Once the European Union passed the EUDPD, Canada also decided to institute its own privacy measures to protect its citizens' data. Known as the Personal Information Protection and Electronic Documents Act (PIPEDA), this new law piggybacks on a 1995 Canadian law instituting privacy standards. As with the GDPR and EUDPD, PIPEDA restricts how businesses are allowed to collect, use, and/or disclose PII of Canadian citizens. All but three Canadian provinces are subject to PIPEDA, though British Columbia, Alberta, and Quebec are bound by privacy and security protections that mimic standard Canadian privacy law.

### Other International Regulations

Since 2001, credit card companies have been operating under the Payment Card Industry Data Security Standard (PCI DSS) and the Cardholder Information Security Program (CISP). It isn't a legal standard but rather an industry standard adopted by the world's two largest credit card companies, Visa and MasterCard. Since the beginning of online transactions, credit cards were necessary to maximize efficient payment processing. Because of that, it was imperative for these two credit card giants to devise standards for payment processing. The standards are used to:

- Protect credit card holders from data leaks and exposure.
- Ensure confidentiality and proper security for consumer information.
- Implement and supply the technology required to protect payment information.
- Unify online payment standards around the globe.

Payment processes governed by the PCI DSS include various financial transactions from automatic teller machine (ATM) withdrawals to point-of-sale (POS) transactions. Businesses utilizing any of these instruments to process payments are required to provide proper firewall protections, encryption, secure authentication, anti-virus protections, and more to comply with PCI DSS standards.

Another industry standard that regulates financial instruments is the International Convergence of Capital Measurement and Capital Standards (ICCMCS), also known as Basel II. Based on recommendations from central bankers from more than a dozen countries, Basel II protects customers, vendors, and end users against risky banking transactions between nations by standardizing capital requirements for international banks.

From a U.S. perspective, most businesses will come up against these privacy regulations more often than others. However, it is important to be aware of some of the data requirements of other countries that have looser and sometimes tighter standards for controlling and/or protecting user data.

For example, there are currently nearly two dozen countries with data localization requirements for information generated within their borders. Others require companies to build data centers locally to prevent data from crossing national borders. Russia is entertaining a law that would mandate local storage of data that must be maintained and stored for at least six months within the country. India requires e-mail hosts to maintain their servers locally.

As discussed in Chapter 1, data localization measures limit Internet freedom and have a detrimental effect on global e-commerce. Doing business in authoritarian nations presents new challenges for complying with regulations governing the Internet. Many of those laws seek to control online activities of citizens and local businesses, unlike European and U.S. laws that strive to protect individual privacy.

## Preparing for Future Regulations

It doesn't matter what size a business is or where it operates; network administrators still have to be fully aware of the many laws governing information stored online and sent and received domestically and abroad. Moreover, there will be many more changes to current regulations in the future. To date, there are more than 80 new privacy laws being enacted across the United States alone. Internationally, laws are being drafted that will change reporting requirements by adding new regulations.

Additionally, new technologies will make updating and adjusting current regulations a necessity going forward. CEOs can't afford to burn out on SOX updates and compliance meetings with their IT departments. All of that is fast becoming part and parcel of how businesses must operate in the 21st century's global economy.

# 4

# Are New Internet Regulations Helping or Hurting Business?

*I do have a political agenda. It's to have as few regulations as possible.*

— FORMER U.S. VICE PRESIDENT DAN QUAYLE[1]

*If you run a corporation, your job is to maximize the return on investment for your investors. Good for you. But by the same token, we have to remember that corporations have no compassion. That's why legislation and regulations are necessary.*

— RUSSELL SIMMONS, HIP-HOP MUSIC ENTREPRENEUR AND ACTIVIST[2]

*We have to encourage the future we want rather than trying to prevent the future we fear.*

— BILL JOY, CO-FOUNDER OF SUN MICROSYSTEMS[3]

THE ABOVE THREE EPIGRAPHS embody the tension between the overarching forces affecting how the Internet is and will be regulated. Too many business executives approach regulations from a combative stance. For them any new regulation is simply a new headache and more red tape they have to clear just to do their jobs. It feels intrusive and unnecessary.

For consumers and citizens around the world, regulations are more necessary now than ever, since many are trusting businesses to protect and keep their personal data safe. Over the past several years, many businesses and governments have failed to protect the data they are entrusted with. As much as businesses hate to deal with new regulations, Russell Simmons's quotation bears repeating: "Corporations have no compassion. That's why legislation and regulations are necessary."

Meanwhile, innovators, consumers, and businesses want the freedom to see what is possible. Once upon a time, the idea of global e-commerce was frightening. Less than 10 percent of the population felt willing to enter credit card information online. Today nearly all citizens in advanced nations expect to get their orders placed and shipped faster and easier by ordering online — using their credit cards!

In other words, if fear had stopped businesses from testing ways to process payments securely online and to provide the logistics necessary to fulfill those orders, there would be no global e-commerce to regulate. The world would still be stuck in a 20th-century economy with 21st-century technology.

Clearly, there has to be a happy medium. Is it possible for regulators to develop policies that protect consumers online while mindfully considering the effects of those laws on business? As for the newest regulations governing the Internet, will they help or hurt global e-commerce?

## Measuring the Effectiveness of New Regulations

By the time this book is read, it is very likely there will be some new regulations already being discussed. Right now there are a slew of regulations coming from every angle of the globe to combat terrorism, cybercrime, IP theft, and more. What are the effects of these new and current regulations? Are they helping or hurting business? Is there evidence either in theory or in practice that they:

- Actually thwart cybercrime?
- Protect nations from fraud and cyberattacks?
- Respect the privacy rights of individuals?
- Make global commerce better?
- Make global commerce safer?
- Help create a useful uniform global standard for business IT management?

When new regulations are examined, it is evident there is no cohesion. Every nation has its own laws at the same time that some nations are bound by international agreements that conflict with individual domestic laws. The result is that these new regulations both help and hurt businesses in different ways.

One of the most important Internet issues that affect businesses around the world is cybercrime. Few international regulations deal with it at all, and it is the sore point for most international agreements attempting to regulate cyberspace. With that in mind, new regulations seem to do little to actually thwart cybercrimes.

## Individuals and Hackers Get Around Regulations

Criminals by nature don't respect laws. Additionally, there are few international laws specifically governing cybercrime. Furthermore, cybercriminals are much harder to trace than other lawbreakers. Part of their modus operandi is to work in the shadows so they can go undetected. Not only do local law-enforcement officers lack the skills to trace professional hackers and cybercriminals but they often don't have the tools to enforce compliance with laws that are basically nonexistent.

For that reason, many cybercrimes go unreported and unprosecuted. Think about it: who would an individual call if his or her computer was hacked? What can local police actually do about it? Where regulations do exist, cybercriminals frequently find easy ways around them. According to the World Health Organization (WHO), being able to buy and receive prescription medicines online makes it possible for cybercriminals to subvert health regulations such as the HIPAA.[4]

Individuals have practically no recourse for pursuing cybercriminals. Intermediary liability often protects businesses from lawsuits, and when Internet thieves are actually traced, the best prosecutors can do is to settle the case. Settlements and class-action suits have the same legal problems any prosecution of cybercrimes has — insufficient laws to deal with this new type of criminal.

Pursuing restitution for victims of cybercrimes ends up being costly and ineffective. It is likely the reason cybercrimes have increased year after year while prosecutions of data theft dropped by 5 percent in 2015.[5]

## Policing International Cybercrimes

U.S. companies and individuals are up against professional hackers from around the world. In fact, the majority of cybercrimes committed in the United States originate from a foreign source. Of all the cyberattacks recorded in 2014, China launched more than 40 percent of them. But who do companies or individuals alert if China sends an attack their way? What can be done?

If we consider that Sony, a major motion picture studio, shut down production of a feature film when North Korea launched a crippling cyberattack against the U.S.-based company, what do small firms and individuals do in the face of increasing cybercriminality?

There are few regulations, and those that exist do little to deter cybercrimes. Fortunately, in September 2015, U.S. President Obama and President Xi Jinping of China struck an agreement to stop supporting and enabling data theft and cyberespionage.[6] As seen in the chart below, since the agreement was forged there has been enormous progress against unauthorized China-based intrusions.

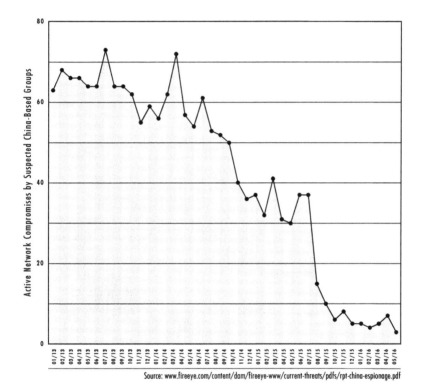

Source: www.fireeye.com/content/dam/fireeye-www/current-threats/pdfs/rpt-china-espionage.pdf

Ironically, tracing nation-to-nation attacks is much easier to do for governments than tracking individual hacks committed by cybercriminals against individuals and corporations. Although both individuals and businesses can and do get attacked by foreign governments, for the most part, businesses are trying to combat the most elusive hackers — anonymous lone wolves and professional criminal hacker rings.

To bring these actors to justice, their locations must first be determined. Then the evidence of the crime has to be established (some ransomware hacks leave little trace of a network intrusion). Finally, if those two goals have been reached, then applicable laws must be found and applied. Again, no real laws with enforcement power exist internationally. The inability to pursue cyber-criminals across borders and the lack of concrete international agreement on how to deal with them will ensure the menace of cybercrime will get worse.

## Ways Regulations Governing the Internet Help Businesses

Protecting businesses varies by industry and business type because the types of cybercriminals attracted to particular companies differ based on the sort of business it is. For example, businesses in the tech industry have to take special precautions to protect their intellectual property and research and develop-ment from data thieves. Businesses are largely responsible for self-protection through best-business practices and industry standards to prevent data theft. Measures such as:

- Bans on outside devices.
- Monitoring employee access to networks.
- Instituting network security protections.
- Strict vetting of vendors and contractors.
- Adopting data security measures.

Now that many of the newest regulations include some data collection and storage restrictions, businesses will have to take even more precautions to keep user data safe. But, in fact, limiting data collection actually helps busi-nesses. Of course, there is a huge qualification that goes with that: some data collection is necessary for business purposes and restrictions that hinder crucial business processes do hurt companies.

Besides the legal consequences of gathering and storing too much consumer data, collecting too much data can make networks less safe. Having to monitor and store huge caches of data that are no longer relevant to day-to-day operations creates vulnerabilities in network protection because it is easier to avoid detection when there is an intrusion that siphons information that is rarely accessed.

When a third party is used for IT management, a monthly fee has to be paid to store data. It might be much less than the fees to maintain IT infra-structure on a daily basis, but it is a wasted expense. Think about the new GDPR that gives European consumers the right not only to prevent companies from collecting and storing data on them but also to request audits and reports detailing the specific data in their systems on individual consumers as well as how it is used. Clearly, the less data kept, the easier it is to comply with regulations governing data storage, use, and collection.

## Ways Regulations Governing the Internet Hurt Businesses

Goals have a lot to do with how regulations are crafted and how businesses respond to them. While some of the laws discussed previously can and do at times hurt businesses, there are regulations in effect and going into effect that are singularly focused on goals that are in direct conflict with business aims:

- A Russian law purportedly aimed at preventing monopolies actually manipulates competition within the country's borders. This law claims to thwart monopolies, but what it does is exactly what American citizens fought hard against in winning the battle on net neutrality — companies can pay to gain greater exposure of their content online.
- Up until recently, China regularly instituted regulations that give its tech companies an unfair advantage over U.S. firms.
- India's telephone companies have begun using regulations to prevent their citizens from accessing Voice over Internet Protocol (VoIP) online tools or charge big fees for using VoIP, which is largely free, to make local and international calls.
- The saying is that the Internet never forgets, but European nations are beginning to demand that search engines do forget. Germany is just one of several European countries that have pushed for greater privacy about past crimes, victim names, and bad press that can be found online, demanding removal of certain types of information.
- Iran blocked Twitter during the Green Revolution a few years ago and continues to prevent Iranian citizens from accessing many parts of the Internet. Twitter, a U.S. company that is one of many in opposition to Iran's censorship laws, is using 2FA to provide end users with a backdoor method for accessing its site. Iran's regulations have nothing to do with data protection for its citizens.

Takedown requests are the number one tactic of authoritarian governments for limiting Internet freedom. In the name of security and individual protections, authoritarian governments request takedowns of information for violations of religious, censorship, and morality laws that free nations couldn't even legally adopt. Yet because of national sovereignty and no uniform global regulatory strategy over the Internet, businesses dealing with consumers in these countries have to comply.

Even the United Kingdom, one of the America's closest and strongest allies, has created a new flagging tool to combat terrorism but could be used to request video takedowns that fall outside that mandate.[7] In the end, any flags coming from government officials are subjective and have the potential to result in reducing Internet freedom and thereby hurting U.K. business interactions with other businesses in the rest of the world.

## Protecting Privacy Helps and Hurts

Since the majority of data sent and received through e-commerce is private and personal, protections to help protect consumers against data theft are very important. Yet if the business ramifications of privacy protection laws aren't fully understood, all the parties involved can be hurt. Too often current privacy regulations focus solely on protecting individual privacy without balancing that need with normal business functions that require some level of data processing.

Seemingly, the solution is simple: weigh privacy laws against business needs for data collection and meet in the middle. However, that is overly simplistic. Consider this: how much data, what type of data, and how long it might need to be stored differ greatly based on the type of company and industry involved. Firms working in the health-care industry that are responsible for maintaining health records have to meet even stricter standards than most other businesses to comply with HIPAA regulations.

Conversely, retailers often benefit from exemptions that allow more cross-border data freedom to speed up order and payment processes. At the same time retailers have suffered some of the most high-profile cyberattacks exposing PII for hundreds of millions of customers worldwide. To that end, regulators are urgently drafting privacy protections that might help safeguard consumer data while making online commerce much more difficult and costly.

## Measures to Protect Privacy Online

One way businesses have attempted to comply with data security regulations is to add encryption tools or to make user data anonymous so that even if hackers gain access to those records they can't glean the PII they want. Data theft becomes harder with both measures but not impossible. All hackers have to do to fill in the blanks is to cross-reference data rendered anonymous with other pertinent PII gathered from different avenues.

Crucial to online commerce is a level of trust. When consumers hand over their PII to businesses, they have to be assured the information will be kept safe. High-profile data hacks shake confidence in businesses to protect consumer data. On top of that, as mentioned before, many national laws concerning online commerce can only be enforced within those nations' borders. There is no overarching global privacy law to which all countries must adhere, which in turn adds to the kind of uncertainty that results in more protectionist laws.

Similar to the way the International Organization for Standardization sets rules for IT managers, the Asia-Pacific Economic Cooperation (APEC) has devised a series of electronic commerce standards for companies that work in the Asia-Pacific region. Created in 1989, APEC now has a roster of 21 countries whose aim is to facilitate trade between and among its members.[8]

## Industry Self-Regulation Versus Government Regulation

Generally speaking, the goals of the APEC Electronic Commerce Steering Group (ECSG) are laudable in the current contentious climate surrounding privacy laws.[9] It encourages cooperation between governments and businesses to meet individual privacy standards that protect consumers. But, as Russell Simmons points out in his epigraph at the beginning of this chapter, businesses are ultimately in business to make money.

The supreme goal for APEC is to make commerce easier, and its primary objective is to help inform regulations that are friendly to business. Based on the "APEC Blueprint for Action on Electronic Commerce," crafted by the organization in 1998, the stated goals of the ECSG are:

- To promote electronic commerce development and use.
- To support legal and regulatory policy creation for APEC member states.
- To develop consistent and transparent regulations and policies.
- To help APEC member states use information technology to enhance economic growth and development.[10]

As a business group, APEC's views about government regulations are more concerned with facilitating business processes than with individual privacy rights. On balance, the organization wants regulatory help establishing global norms and at the same time would like governments to create a business-friendly climate when developing privacy regulations — two aims that are often at odds.

Most important from a business perspective is for government regulations to remain neutral, or put another way, for governments to create regulations that do no harm. For that reason, many businesses and business groups prefer self-regulation to government control while realizing the necessity to comply with national and international rules governing e-commerce. In 2014 APEC began assisting its members with EUDPD compliance involving cross-border data rules.

In 2015 APEC petitioned the European Union to accept its Cross Border Privacy Rules (CBPR) certification as a way to meet EU Binding Corporate Rules (BCRs). While the European Union expressed interest in the idea and continues to meet with the group, to date no agreement has been forged. APEC is also attempting to help liable data processors get in front of data privacy regulations contained in the GDPR and EUDPD.

## Protecting Intellectual Property Helps and Hurts

For those who work in research and development, intellectual property protections are paramount to secure confidential business information. Seemingly, IP protections should only help businesses. However, online news sites and businesses, even ordinary people posting pictures and memes on social media, can be held in violation of IP regulations if those protections are too onerous.

Right now someone can share a video on a personal blog post that can technically be classified as copyright infringement. According to the law, the content shared is the intellectual property of the creator or originator. But because most IP laws, in the United States at least, protect intermediaries from lawsuits and give IP owners the right to remove copyrighted data that is used illegally online, business can continue as usual without stifling or hurting Internet freedom.

Researchers, as mentioned earlier, have to access the IP of others frequently in the course of their work. Scientists in a biopharmaceutical firm, for example, need to cross-reference the studies and works of researchers outside their company to receive Food and Drug Administration (FDA) approval for certain experiments they conduct concerning a new product. How many new and innovative drugs would be stopped dead in their tracks if a company had to pay usage fees to access dozens, sometimes hundreds, of sources that contain protected IP?

On the other hand, Google, IBM, Microsoft, and most tech companies depend on strong IP regulations to protect their proprietary information from business competitors. So far, on the consumer side, U.S. regulations have been broad enough to allow for fair use that doesn't slow down or impede online users from innovating, but carve out stronger protections for certain proprietary IP for businesses. Is it enough? Most tech leaders would probably say no. The fact that major tech firms are under constant assault from foreign and domestic competitors trying to steal their IP explains why large tech firms are pushing for even stronger IP protections, while consumers are generally happy with the way things are.

## Data Localization Could Help but Mostly Hurts

Data localization has become a dirty word for proponents of a free and unfettered cyberspace. For both individuals and businesses, it has the potential to make global e-commerce much more difficult and expensive. It can provide an unfair advantage for local businesses, and in its most restrictive form, it can act as a trade barrier.

So how do data localization regulations help? Their goal is to protect national IT infrastructure from online intrusions from actors outside a nation's border. Data is most vulnerable in transit, and when it moves from one country's network to another nation's system, there are opportunities for bad actors to intercept it. Moreover, U.S. companies are storing PII for hundreds of millions of consumers around the world.

Again, the news that the National Security Agency (NSA) had been collecting data and spying on allies and enemies alike is largely the impetus for data localization rules. The feeling is that if companies must store PII locally, then the country where those citizens reside can protect that data better and safeguard those individuals from spying. Evidence doesn't back up that theory. To the contrary, many experts believe that data localization might have the opposite effect make data less secure.

Case in point: how can cloud providers reasonably monitor and protect business data if they aren't allowed to store that information? The cloud, by nature, is ubiquitous. It is location-less. To create data localization regulations when cloud computing and wireless technology is the norm is on the whole counterproductive. And data localization laws require businesses to build data centers in the countries where they operate.

Think about cloud service providers that have customers all over the world. The costs would be too exorbitant to build data centers in every location where they operate. Co-localization is helping businesses get around these rules, but it is still an added expense that negates at least some of the cost savings cloud computing provides.

## Combative Relationship Between Governments and Businesses Mostly Hurts

While the European Union has made privacy protection a priority that exceeds U.S. standards, when it comes to net neutrality the United States leads the way in creating a climate that benefits online users — a move that tech firms dependent on users accessing their websites are hugely behind. At the same time U.S. wireless phone carriers and cable providers are vehemently opposed to rules that limit their ability to charge more for faster online service.

The European Union has passed its own version of net neutrality rules that many argue leaves too many ways for EU businesses to get around those regulations. If they do, users in the European Union could wind up being shut out of parts of the Internet unless they pay more for access. The law explicitly prohibits creating what are called fast lanes online, but businesses are exempted from the law when providing "specialized services," an exemption that many expect telecom companies to employ to create fast lanes under the guise of specialized services.[11]

This push and pull is just one example of the combative stance many businesses take toward government regulations. In June 2016, a federal appeals court upheld the Federal Communications Commission's ruling of the previous year that wireless phone service and Internet access are both now considered public utilities.[12] As such the FCC has banned blocking, throttling, and paid prioritization (accepting fees for favored treatment, i.e., creating fast lanes) by broadband providers.

On one hand, the FCC ruling is a huge victory for users and proponents of a free and unfettered Internet. On the other hand, the decision will fuel further fighting that is expected to go all the way to the Supreme Court. In the eyes of telecom companies, the government is overreaching. Just as in the Apple case in February 2016 in which the Federal Bureau of Investigation (FBI) sought and won a court order to force Apple to crack the code locking the cell phone of terrorists who committed a murderous attack in San Bernardino, California, in late 2015, business and the government are at cross-purposes.

## Oppressive Content Takedowns Only Hurt

Americans haven't experienced the type of content takedowns many citizens around the world face. In many authoritarian countries, IT compliance means adhering to laws that are in stark contrast to American values as well as those of many other Western nations or else have content taken down or websites blocked. Some governments send requests to take down content in the manner of the new EU "right to be forgotten" law. Oppressive regimes, however, can unilaterally take down content, sometimes without citizens realizing it because the governments aren't required to inform them or request their compliance.

Another problem with these types of content takedowns is that there is often no rhyme or reason for them. Sometimes governments use local censorship or morality laws to take down content based on rules that aren't explicitly codified or known. Some takedowns are simply a disguised effort to create an uneven playing field for foreign competitors by taking down content on flimsy charges.

Google as well as other U.S. companies were willing to forgo the lucrative Chinese market rather than comply with what the companies deemed unfair and discriminatory content takedowns, although Google has since relented and created versions of its search engine that comply with more stringent content and censorship rules.

When companies are subject to these types of takedowns, it hurts their business operations in a number of ways. It dissuades users from accessing foreign sites, giving an unfair advantage to local providers even if users prefer the foreign sites. It also hurts business growth by preventing small and start-up businesses from competing. One study has shown that almost 80 percent of businesses surveyed suffered because of censorship.[13] Online commerce is hindered and Internet service becomes spotty and slow overall. The problem is only worsening with takedowns increasing sharply over the past two years.

## Complications Arising from Regulations on Cloud Computing

As if regulations weren't troublesome enough, when the rise of cloud computing is factored in, the complications get even more substantial. For instance, cloud computing and service providers offering cloud technology will bump into regulations that affect:

- How network architecture is structured.
- How user identities are protected.
- How network access is managed.
- How data protection protocols are implemented and enforced.
- How breaches are reported.

Now multiply the above by the number of laws governing IT compliance in each state and country that cloud providers operate in and dramatic change can easily be seen in the responsibilities of network and IT managers.

Perhaps the greatest problem confronting network managers is the issue of data localization. Fortunately for publicly traded U.S. companies, if they are in full compliance with SOX regulations, they will also meet the standards for several other U.S. laws governing reporting standards for IT compliance.[14]

| Reports | GLBA | HIPAA | PCI-DSS | SOX |
|---|:---:|:---:|:---:|:---:|
| User logon/logoff | ● | ● | ● | ● |
| Logon failure | ● | ● | ● | ● |
| Audit logs access | ● | ● | ● | ● |
| Object access | | ● | ● | ● |
| System events | | ● | | ● |
| Host session status | | ● | | ● |
| Security log archiving | ● | ● | | ● |
| Track account management and use group changes | | | | ● |
| Track audit policy changes | | | ● | ● |
| Successful user account validation | | ● | | ● |
| Unsuccessful use account validation | | ● | | ● |
| Track individual user actions report | | | ● | ● |
| Track application access | | | | ● |
| Source: https://jisajournal.springeropen.com/articles/10.1186/s13174-016-0046-8#Sec6 | | | | |

On this score, industry standards are a better guide for counteracting threats to networks than most government regulations. For example, ISO guidelines can help cloud service providers structure networks that combat typical malicious intrusions coming from denial of service (DoS) attacks and other malware. Currently, there are no regulations to fight one of the newest threats facing consumers and businesses — ransomware that hijacks networks. There is also no regulation to thwart internal sabotage of networks, but most business IT policies, particularly for companies in the tech industry, have their own protocols for preventing these types of network insecurities and vulnerabilities.

## Hybrid Cloud Systems Complicate Regulatory Compliance

Because many businesses, around half of them, are opting for a hybrid cloud solution as opposed to a total cloud solution, regulatory compliance is made even more difficult. Hybrid solutions keep part of a company's sensitive data in-house under company control while other functions are outsourced to third-party service providers. This presents enormous challenges for internal IT departments responsible for managing compliance and for cloud service providers that are only charged with managing certain parts of a business's overall IT networks.

## Open Discussions Help Make Regulations Better

Because data protection for individual users has become part of the overall discussion about Internet governance around the world, these regulations will have a better chance to succeed. Now that the United States has won a victory on net neutrality, that triumph will help citizens in other countries where there is no such rule. In order to continue dealing with the United States, countries wishing to provide access to American websites and businesses must respect U.S. net neutrality rules. In the same way, European data protection laws will require U.S. companies to increase privacy rights, at the very least for their European trading partners.[15]

Knee-jerk reactions to data theft and online espionage that are causing some nations to consider or adopt data localization laws bring to the forefront the conflict inherent in those types of regulatory solutions. Free and unfettered e-commerce in a globally connected world can't abide stringent location restrictions for sending, receiving, processing, and storing data across borders. The very nature of global e-commerce implies the need for the free flow of cross-border data.

Balancing the need to ensure safer and more secure networks for governments, businesses, and individuals from country to country with the need to continue to encourage global free trade requires open discussions. It involves weighing the benefits of such measures against the costs. Keep in mind that regulations governing data protections aren't limited to what are considered large businesses. Any business is subject to these new regulations, and violations have varying and at times quite stiff penalties for violations. Coming up with regulations that increase security will require a global solution that begins with the types of discussions these regulatory changes are bringing about.

# 5

## The Cost of Protectionism on Global E-Commerce

*When America closes its doors, so does everybody else. We are the primary engine of growth in the world and we are the only beacon of free trade left, and open markets.*

— FORMER UTAH GOVERNOR JON HUNTSMAN, JR.[1]

*There is no more precious currency than the unfettered liberty to explore while engaged in an "Idea Economy." You cannot centrally plan the "Idea Economy" any more than you can plan fun or spontaneity. Regulations are restraints in an "Idea Economy." The entrepreneur is either free to experiment or not.*

— A.E. SAMAAN, AUTHOR AND ARTIST[2]

*The "Idea Economy" is a conversation. Try to channel or control that conversation and you will stop the chatter.*

— A.E. SAMAAN, AUTHOR AND ARTIST[3]

THE GLOBAL ECONOMY IS NOW AN "IDEA ECONOMY," to use a term coined by Hewlett-Packard.[4] A brilliant idea can turn an average everyday citizen into a multi-millionaire overnight. The Internet has created a global marketplace that has seeded this fertile ground for innovative ideas to flourish. Now, however, protectionist measures threaten the very idea of an Idea Economy.

Perhaps what is needed is for more individuals, businesses, and governments to think about what the end result of these protectionist measures will mean for global e-commerce. The trillions of dollars of new revenue, the widening of the global middle class, and the Internet's extraordinary ability to lift people out of poverty could all be lost due to shrinking Internet access and thus e-commerce overall.

Those are the costs of protectionism for global e-commerce, but there are more. If the costs over the long term are better understood, then maybe a global solution can be found.

The Idea Economy refers to the way in which knowledge itself has become an economic driver and money-making industry. Software makers provide tools that use data analytics to drive more business for which many companies are willing to pay top dollar. And it refers to the fact that the traditional behemoths of industry, even in the tech arena, no longer own the fast lane in an Idea Economy.

Little players become giant players and giant players can become antiquated in the rapidly advancing age of technology. Today's economy places enormous value on innovation. New systems, new governments, and new technologies all create new problems, and people are needed with the expertise to manage the problems they create. The more innovative and nimble a business is the greater advantage it has in today's marketplace.

Enter new regulations on top of protectionist measures with the potential to stifle that speed and creativity, which translates into real dollar costs to businesses around the globe. What are those costs and is it possible to move nations away from protectionism for the sake of preserving what is good about the opportunities created by global e-commerce?

## The Global Economy Creates New Opportunities for Innovation

The Internet is responsible for starting the rapid advancement of human knowledge happening today. At its inception it produced a doubling of human knowledge on a nearly annual basis. The following decade saw human knowledge doubling on average every year and a half.

According to researchers at IBM, technology alone will soon shrink the time it takes for human knowledge to double to half a day because of the IoT and the technology developed around it.[5] This rapid advance of knowledge is why technology is changing and evolving so fast. Businesses have a hard time keeping up. It is the freedom to experiment that leads to new innovations. The Idea Economy is helping individuals and businesses around the globe think outside the box to come up with inventive and amazing ways to make commerce and life in general more convenient.

For regulators the speed of innovation renders it nearly impossible to devise good legislation that continues to fuel experimentation and innovation while protecting consumers, businesses, and governments from the dangers new technologies present. As technology has gone from the desktop to cell phones and now to the IoT and machine-to-machine (M2M) devices, the challenge of securing data grows just as rapidly.

Disruptive businesses such as Uber and Netflix necessitate new ways to imagine the global economy.[6] Blockbuster no longer exists because of Netflix. Before, we had to physically go to a video store to rent a movie. Today we can stream virtually any film from the old to the newest release without ever leaving the comfort of home. Protectionist laws could prevent new businesses from ever being realized and could squelch the ability of these new industries to function.

## Regulatory Hurdles for Disruptive Businesses

Why is Uber better than catching a cab and Airbnb luring people away from typical hotel bookings? It is because these new disruptive businesses provide those same services cheaper, and in Uber's case faster. Airbnb makes hoteliers out of individuals with spare rooms to rent, while Uber transforms people with time and transport into drivers. Wherever customers are Uber drivers can get to them in a few minutes, whereas a taxi might take half an hour to forty-five minutes. Renting a room or a house for the weekend through Airbnb can be cheaper and cozier than a cookie-cutter hotel room. The proof is in the billions of dollars these businesses bring in each year now.

These innovative businesses are a win for consumers, too. One estimate puts the number at $3.5 billion for how much money consumers saved on transportation and hotel stays by using Uber, Lyft (another private car service), and Airbnb. Over 10 million people chose an Airbnb over a hotel in its first six years of existence from 2007 through 2013.[7] As the popularity of these services has grown, so has the need to regulate them. Uber in particular faces regulatory hurdles around the world, not just in the United States, as does Airbnb.[8]

- Uber came to Austin, Texas, in 2014, and two years later in May 2016 a referendum demanding that Uber drivers adhere to many of the same regulations governing cab drivers, like fingerprinting for all drivers, was passed overwhelmingly.[9] As a result, Uber decided to end its services in Austin rather than submit to city regulations.
- In New York, Airbnb has come under scrutiny for violating the state's

zoning laws. According to the Attorney General's Office, more than 70 percent of the rooms rented through the site didn't meet New York State regulatory standards for rentals.

- Germany didn't outright ban Airbnb but instead mandated that in order to provide short-term rentals individuals must seek permission from the government to do so.

- Two years ago Paris enacted a law that requires Airbnb providers to allow inspections of rentals prior to offering space due to suspicions that many Airbnb rentals were illegal.

- Massachusetts is part of a class-action suit against Uber for violating employment laws by erroneously classifying its drivers as independent contractors so that it doesn't have to provide employee benefits.

Canada hasn't banned Uber nationally, but several cities have done so, as have regulators in Frankfurt, Germany. Like many new and emerging technologies, these new business models create inconsistency across the board. Customers can access Uber in certain parts of the country but not in others or certain parts of a state but not in others. Once considered niche businesses, the sheer size and rapid growth of the sharing economy or peer-to-peer (P2P) economy has spurred cities and states around the globe to consider how to develop strategies for dealing with these disruptive businesses.

## New Opportunities Create More Global Wealth

Before cloud computing and the IoT even began exploding over the past few years, e-commerce between businesses around the world made up the vast majority of the more than $16 trillion of revenue generated from online transactions — a whopping 90 percent! Over the next year as M2M and IoT technology continue to revolutionize business-to-business interactions, the numbers are predicted to soar even higher. That is because as M2M technology is combined with the IoT, the value created for businesses could quadruple from close to $45 billion five years ago to almost $300 billion by the end of 2017.

In fact, it is very likely that those two technologies, which add computing capability to machines and devices, will largely be focused on improving business operations more than adding value for consumers. For instance, drone technology and driverless vehicles could make deliveries faster for consumers. But for the businesses making those deliveries, M2M technology and automation will add value from top to bottom — from radio-frequency identification (RIFD) sensors to track goods to big-data analytics driving sales and marketing strategies.

Overall global e-commerce has lifted the economic status of individuals around the world, creating a new global middle class. New opportunities are arising for highly skilled and knowledgeable IT workers, while even blue-collar jobs are being created for data managers and operators of advanced technology.

## Ways Growing Protectionism Could Hurt Global E-Commerce

With all of the clear advantages brought about by the global economy, protectionism, perhaps more than any regulation out there, threatens to slow down or stop these new opportunities and the wealth creation that results from it. Think about this: just three years ago online retail transactions that crossed borders amounted to more than $100 billion.[10] Since then those numbers have only grown. Imperative to enabling that kind of cross-border commerce is the freedom to send and receive data over networks that expand beyond national borders. How those transactions were completed was through an international payment system that enables a consumer in the Far East to order goods online from a company in the U.S. Midwest.

Mechanisms for making payments come in different forms from PayPal, to Google Wallet, to credit card payments. Add to the mix bitcoins and the ability to legally sign documents with an e-signature and the need for free cross-border data flow is obvious.

Yet what has been happening over the past two years is a move around the globe to cordon off cross-border data at the edges of nations. If that occurs, what happens to online commerce, which contributes billions to societies around the globe?

## Dangers of Cross-Border Data Restrictions

Cross-border data restrictions hinder more than just online commerce. Streaming videos online, accessing social media, shipping and receiving goods, even working together in research and development or non-governmental organizations (NGOs) with other nations around the world is affected by cross-border data restrictions. So why would countries that clearly benefit from the free flow of online commerce be willing to sacrifice those gains? It is all in the name of data protection and national security.

Only 5 percent of U.S. businesses that export their goods outside the

Internet deal with countries on multiple continents. Nearly all (95 percent) of eBay businesses, which are made up of many small and midsized companies, conduct business on four or more continents. On YouTube more than 80 percent of users watching videos don't live in the United States and are accessing that data across borders. Much of the worldwide economic gains and the growing global middle class is the result of small and medium-sized enterprises (SMEs) building up their businesses on the backs of a growing and international customer base.

New businesses such as Airbnb and Uber depend on the Internet to function, and data collection, payment processing, and more are necessary cross-border data flows for that business model to work. The creation of new forms of online payments assists people living in regions where access to credit cards and bank accounts is scarce. The World Bank estimated back in 2014 that nearly half the world's population doesn't have credit cards and bank accounts.

## Ten Ways Protectionism Threatens Global E-Commerce

Of course, there are many potential dangers inherent in these new online payment processes that give rise to legitimate concerns about cross-border data flows. The potential for online theft increases when users send and receive financial information online. Right now the onus is on businesses to safeguard that data, something that has been a struggle over the past few years even for seemingly impenetrable networks.

Not all data flow restrictions — some could reasonably argue most — aren't intended to be protectionist in spirit, but without a smart strategy that clarifies and sets reasonable expectations for how online commerce works best that is the effect in practice.

**1. Prevents Common Ground for Uniform Policymaking:** Probably the most ardent proponents of uniform policies regulating the Internet are U.S. businesses. However, businesses are mostly interested in crafting policies that will ultimately help strengthen U.S. dominance in cyberspace.[11] On the other side of the coin, countries such as China and India are more inclined to institute protectionist measures to help their burgeoning tech industries, for example, compete, which in turn prevents finding common ground.

**2. Closes Protectionist Governments (and Their Citizens) Out of the Global Economy:** When dealing with nations that share U.S. values, working to find areas of common ground are much more possible than in closed societies where protectionist measures are primarily a means to control the population. To the detriment of people in large regions of the world where citizens are completely shut out of the global economy, any moves toward global e-commerce can't be made.

**3. Government Intrusion Thwarts Foreign Investment:** Google's exit from the Chinese market a few years ago was explicitly due to what it felt was constant government intrusion into its business. Whether through censorship or anti-terrorism laws, too much government intrusion thwarts foreign investment in areas that would otherwise benefit from the financial gains garnered from global e-commerce.

**4. Creates Geographical Barriers to Trade:** As areas with onerous protectionist Internet regulations continue to push more and more businesses out, in essence, those measures result in geographical trade barriers. Brexit and the new GDPR cross-border data regulations could potentially create geographical trade barriers to the detriment of global e-commerce within the European Union and United Kingdom.

**5. Prevents Broad Sharing of Information and Entertainment:** Adding to the worrisome trends coming from the European Commission are new rules that restrict information sharing and adds new copyright protections that could stifle innovation. Moreover, an announcement in 2016 shows the potential disruption these new protectionist measures could have:

- New regulatory proposals governing online platforms that require websites to "promote more European-created content."[12]
- New protections against hate speech, violence, and pornography that could fine violators, which could potentially include content on U.S. platforms protected as free speech.
- Confidentiality rules governing telecom services could be extended to online communications.
- Doubling down on intermediary liability rules expressed in the EUDPD to enforce compliance.
- Efforts to protect cross-border data for consumers through more transparency and more secure eID to prevent user PII from being stolen.

On the plus side, the European Union intends to make the expiring "free flow of data initiative" more business-friendly for cloud providers and online platform hosts.

**6. Leads Nations to Create Onerous Regulations:** If one nation begins instituting protectionist measures, so do others. The domino effect that protectionist measures have on global e-commerce not only leads to more onerous regulations but it in turn results in an even more incoherent international regulatory environment.

**7. Interferes with Fair Competition:** One of the most distasteful protectionist measures are those that purport to be regulations to protect a country's citizens and businesses but in actuality are only aimed at giving an advantage to domestic companies over foreign competitors. This has a big effect on competition inside and outside a country's borders. Instead of competing on merits, users are often left with an inferior product or service.

**8. Enhances Oppressive Governments' Abusive Powers:** Oppressive governments where authoritarianism allows abuse of power to go unchecked are finding new ways to monitor and control their populations under the guise of user protection. When governments ban certain websites and black out news sites from foreign sources, they are exerting power that prevents their people from fighting back. State-run media sites and news outlets ensure their populations are only fed a steady diet of anti-foreign propaganda, which in turn isolates those countries from the global economy.

**9. Limits Developed Nations' Ability to Grow:** To date there are approximately four billion people around the world without access to the Internet.[13] Whether through lack of infrastructure investment, government restrictions, or the lack of technology, without Internet access, developed nations can't attain the economic gains that global e-commerce has brought about. It is only equal to education as an economic driver of poverty reduction. Innovation, wealth creation, and poverty alleviation are acutely needed in developing nations, and any protectionist laws only further hinder their growth.

## Internet Infrastructure Around the World

Internet accessibility can be measured by how many people are served
by each Internet exchange point (IXP). The lower the number, the better the access.

**Millions of people served by each IXP**

| | |
|---|---|
| South Asia | 215 |
| Sub-Saharan Africa | 49 |
| Middle East & North Africa | 47 |
| East Asia & Pacific | 36 |
| Latin America & Caribbean | 17 |
| Europe & Central Asia | 6 |
| North America | 4 |

Source: International Telecommunications Union, Packet Clearing House, World Bank, World Development Indicators

**10. Further Restricts Global Internet Access:** With more than half the global population living without the Internet, even modest protectionism has an enormous effect on overall access. Even in countries with limited public Internet access, businesses and government agencies still have connectivity to the Internet. For those countries, protectionist measures are largely aimed at tilting the competitive field in favor of their national industries. However, the outcome of such measures can result in even less Internet access in those regions.

## Creating the Legal Global Framework to Encourage E-Commerce

The above 10 ways bring to the fore a fundamental question pertinent to all businesses and governments operating around the globe. Is a legal global framework possible that can encourage e-commerce while also protecting online users? Whatever legal framework that is developed will need to rest on a clearly defined set of guiding principles that answer the concerns of all parties involved from top to bottom.

## A More Secure Internet

Consumers and Internet users don't care that much about how their goods and services are delivered online as long as they can trust that their information is being protected. This helps businesses provide the type of secure connections that will engender trust in their consumers, giving them confidence that whenever they input their credit card information every measure has been taken to keep that data out of the hands of online thieves. Making those measures as consistent and uniform as possible will aid compliance and ensure a more secure Internet for everybody.

## Allowing the Free Flow of Data

Without question in order for global e-commerce to continue to thrive, there has to be an agreement on allowing the free flow of data. There are instances in which some data restrictions make sense, for example, when it comes to the national security apparatuses of governments. But for business, regulations like those proposed by the GDPR should balance the altruistic goals of protecting user data with the efficiency of normal online data flows.

## A Means to Settle Disputes

Possibly the hardest area of agreement is going to be developing a means for dispute resolution. How do businesses combat unfair protectionist measures? Again, because the Internet operates largely irrespective of location at the user end, jurisdiction becomes the biggest hurdle for devising a working framework for settling disputes. Yet to move nations away from protectionist measures, any new regulations need to have oversight with the authority to enforce compliance.

In the absence of regulatory policy, industry leaders have led the way to facilitate global e-commerce. In the same way, some online businesses have created their own internal processes for settling disputes. The best solutions, going forward, will be the result of coordination among industry professionals, businesses, and governments. Already some countries and cities are trying to come up with ways to enable the innovation creating many new disruptive businesses to continue and grow:

- In response to Airbnb, Amsterdam in the Netherlands was the first to pass regulations that actually invite this new business as opposed to hindering it.
- San Francisco also approached Airbnb in a spirit of cooperation by

instituting regulations that okay these types of rentals provided by
residents of the city as long as the proper taxes are collected.

- The United Kingdom is more than welcoming to these new industries
going as far as to announce the goal to make the country the friendliest
environment for businesses in the "sharing economy."

Even car rental giants such as Hertz and Avis are positioning themselves
within the sharing economy and are striving to create their own versions of
Uber. When the new disruptive companies and their traditional competitors work together to devise solutions that aren't solely business-friendly or
user-friendly, they see the most success. Regulations, going forward, will be
necessary to ensure these businesses operate safely and in a way that protects
consumers, which could raise the enormous cost reductions that have given
them the ability to grow.

# 6

# Business Abroad in a Changing IT Regulatory Environment

*You can get to oppression through regulation, especially in an "Idea Economy" which necessitates liberty of the mind to explore.*

— A.E. SAMAAN, AUTHOR AND ARTIST[1]

*Well, basically, the myth is that America has been founded on the free market; the government has done very little; it has thrived under free trade. But actually, if you look at the history, this is actually the country that has succeeded most with protectionist policies.*

— HA-JOON CHANG, ECONOMIST[2]

*Technological errors made by government, industry [DDT, ABM, SST, CIA, etc.] are those of children, who, even though they don't know what the score is, go on playing pre-technological games of power and profit.*

— JOHN CAGE, COMPOSER[3]

**W**ITH ALL OF THE REGULATIONS on the books today and coming online over the next few years, company CIOs are becoming more important than ever in the functions of a business. No longer is doing business abroad exclusive to large multinational corporations. Small and midsized businesses of all kinds are operating in states across the United States and abroad. Managing IT compliance is going to take a concerted effort that brings top-level executives into the decision-making process for how IT networks are structured and managed.

What is possible and what is legal are going to vary greatly from region to region. Protectionism and regulations are both colliding to make network managers' jobs that much harder. In order to be prepared for this new and changing regulatory environment, the skill sets companies are looking for in IT professionals will have to change.

CIOs who are fluent in network management but are totally clueless about regulations governing how their companies send, receive, store, and secure data is no longer sufficient. To ensure that IT policies are in compliance, especially for businesses operating abroad, it is important to understand and anticipate what problems might arise in the future. They aren't all privacy-related and some challenges have very little to do with codified regulations. Knowing the culture around Internet technology in certain locations abroad is crucial to conducting business legally in foreign countries.

Difficulties can be expected operating a business in some foreign markets if IT is managed the same way as it is in the United States. It doesn't matter what type of business or what size it is, IT regulations can't be avoided, and not only are they varied around the world and across America but they also constantly change.

Another problem encountered lately is democracies that typically side with the United States in pushing for a wide-open Internet that now institute protectionist measures. As well, authoritarian governments are exerting control over their countries' Internet users by shifting the onus onto foreign companies to self-censor.

Some companies choose to comply with the demands of their host countries despite those rules and regulations being in direct conflict with their firms' values. Others select where to locate based on more than just the potential customer base. They weigh the cost benefits of investing in new markets where protectionism negates many of the positives to be gained through business investment and expansion.

## Dangers of Internet Protectionism by Democracies on Global Business

It could be argued that the way the Internet spread throughout the world created an imbalance that favored open democracies over nondemocratic countries. In doing so, democracies laid the foundation for global e-commerce but also helped to tilt the playing field by promoting laws that helped make cross-border data flows easier. Entry into foreign markets was facilitated by lax policies giving special tax treatment to lure investment in those markets.[4]

Trade barriers and tariffs were reduced or eliminated as were regulations that ensured best practices. Perhaps that was necessary to produce the global economy of today.

Regardless, it is clear the function of the global economy over the past two decades has been modeled and set by democracies. Those democracies then began pressing for even more Internet expansion by forging trade agreements with nondemocratic nations. To secure the cooperation of nondemocratic nations, the undemocratic ways those countries managed their national IT infrastructures had to be overlooked.

That brings us to today's environment in which democracies are reeling back and second-guessing the wisdom of having an Internet as unfettered for business as it is now. Instead of compelling undemocratic countries to adhere to higher standards, democracies faced with online insecurity, distrust, and trade imbalances have put up their own trade barriers and protectionist regulations. So what happens to businesses operating around the globe?

## Trade Imbalances That Lead to Protectionism

No nation is immune to the current protectionist streak girdling the globe. In fact, as stated earlier, the United States alone is weighing over 80 new measures that would add more layers of regulations imposing tighter rules on trade and data protection. According to the Global Trade Index, since 2008, countries around the world have instituted more than 5,000 protectionist measures that act as trade barriers.[5]

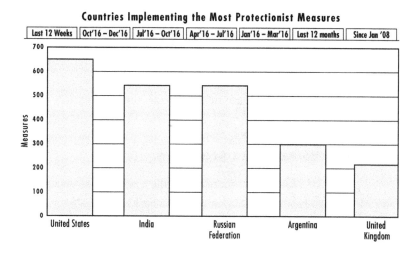

U.S. companies could argue that the relaxing of these rules and the expansion of the Internet has led to enormous growth for the nations that have adopted e-commerce trade rules. On the other hand, others could argue that the United States is responsible for the loose regulation of financial markets that led to the global economic crisis in 2007–08 and the trade imbalances created by lower tariffs and the elimination of trade barriers. All of those measures were necessary for the United States to pursue a global strategy that opened up so many new markets and aided the U.S. economic success.[6]

As much as the philosophy of expansion helped the United States and its trading partners grow, there have also been many downsides that up until now many countries were willing to overlook — things like the massive outsourcing of jobs to low-wage nations and the importation of cheap goods. In fact, the United States has long argued that China manipulates its currency thereby creating an unfair advantage that has resulted in a huge trade deficit between China and America.

Low-wage nations such as China don't have to contend with minimum-wage laws and worker protections that most democracies must. That in itself creates a trade imbalance that favors China. Those imbalances haven't gone unnoticed by U.S. corporations or the American people. Pew Research conducted a study in 2015 surveying American opinions on free trade and found:

- Close to 90 percent of Americans blame China for U.S. job losses.
- Ninety percent rank it as a "very serious issue."
- Less than half of Americans believe NAFTA helped the U.S. economy.[7]

At the same time economists by and large conclude that free trade over time is a good thing, notwithstanding the countries that suffer from imbalances or reap little benefits from these global arrangements. However, to those who live in or operate a business in countries that see little economic benefit from current trade agreements, instituting protectionist measures only makes sense.

## Complying with Restrictive Access Laws

China's population is about four times that of the United States, making the former an extremely attractive consumer market for businesses. Nonetheless, when operating in China, businesses have to make a decision whether or not to comply with that nation's world-famous Great Firewall.

At first Google was among the many U.S. tech giants willing to comply with China's restrictive Internet access laws, altering its services in sometimes creative ways to conform to those restrictions. Then, in 2010, Google chose principle over profit when it exited the Chinese market after suspicions that China itself had launched a cyberattack against Google as well as at several human-rights activists.[8] The result for any country opting to withdraw or risk being shut out of the Chinese market means cutting off an enormous revenue stream reaching into the billions of dollars.[9]

| Losses Are High for U.S. Tech Firms That Have Withdrawn or Been Banned from China | | | |
|---|---|---|---|
| Revenue comparison for major Internet companies, China vs U.S., 2014 (U.S. $ millions) | | | |
| Paid search revenue | | Display advertising revenue | |
| Baidu (China) | 7,644.0 | Sina Weibo (China) | 334.2 |
| Google (U.S.) | 17,811.2 | Facebook (U.S. & Canada) | 5,285.0 |
| | | | Source: IHS Tecnology |

But China and similar authoritarian governments aren't the only ones with restrictive laws that foreign businesses have to be aware of to stay in compliance. For instance, *Freedom House* judged EU nations as the most protective when it came to hate speech.[10] In America posting a picture of a swastika on Facebook isn't illegal, since it is protected by the First Amendment. However, in Germany it is illegal, and as such, Germany has petitioned Facebook to institute more stringent rules against hate speech and imagery within that country.

The "right to be forgotten" law is another restriction in the European Union, making it necessary for companies to comply with data protection rules that aren't required in the United States and weren't necessary when dealing with European countries previously. Recent terrorist attacks in France and other parts of the eurozone have spurred those nations to institute policies that allow takedowns when there is a suspicion that terrorists are posting propaganda or recruiting terrorists. That means companies with a social media presence must make accommodations for those regulations on their EU platforms.

In Russia a company might have to remove comments or content from its website that speak "ill of public officials" or else be sued. In Turkey people can go to jail if someone in authority feels they are "insulting Turkishness." The *Freedom House* survey reported takedowns, deletion requests, blocked content, or user detentions for a variety of different confounding reasons.[11]

Out of the 65 countries surveyed, the greatest number of nations restricted access for reasons such as:

- Forty-seven countries blocked or censored content because of criticism lodged at governments or royal families.
- Twenty-eight countries censored websites or users that tried to report on corruption issues.
- Twenty-three countries used Internet access restrictions and censorship to silence their political opponents.
- Twenty-three countries blocked content about government authorities that was ironic or satirical in nature.
- Twenty-one countries censured websites for content that spoke out on social issues in their nations.
- Twenty-one countries censored content that was deemed blasphemous.

Speaking out for gay rights, standing up for minorities, reporting on violence, or promoting causes that elicit protests and activism either in traditional media or online can get a company expelled from the country in question or result in its Internet content being blocked. Some nations force the companies that host the content to self-censor to hide the fact they are censoring their people, and many companies comply. Not all these laws are even on the books. Restrictions can be arbitrary. They can change from day to day, depending on what is happening in the country. But is it worth the investment given the oppressive environments of some nations?

In 2016 Google re-entered the Chinese market and now adheres to that country's online restrictions. Apple competes with two domestic mobile phone manufacturers in China that are backed by the Chinese government, and yet the company has thrived in that market because of its willingness to comply with China's restrictions. By partnering with China's state-run mobile provider and linking Apple Pay with China's state-run Union Pay bank card, Apple has been able to function quite well within the country. Apple even denied the Chinese government access to its source code without losing any of its privileges, though in early 2016, China removed iBooks and iMovies from a list of accessible content.[12]

All companies will have to think long and hard before deciding to expand to countries such as China, calculating whether or not the risk is worth the reward. Google can get away with altering its services to fit cultural demands, but what about firms that run cloud services? How will those types of regulations hurt how they monitor and store data? Keep in mind that even in

Canada and the United Kingdom there are proposals on data localization. Is it even possible to operate a business while complying with those types of restrictions?

## Small and Medium-Sized Enterprises (SMEs) Liable for Compliance, Too

Talking about big tech giants might make some small and medium-sized enterprises (SMEs) think their little cloud services are too tiny to really be affected by restrictive access laws aimed at competing with U.S. tech giants, but that would be wrong. Global e-commerce has made it possible for businesses large and small to succeed internationally. The Internet allows SMEs to save enormous amounts of cash on overhead and investment costs by not having to expand physically to other countries.

Since monitoring and adhering to ever-changing Internet regulations require the type of knowledge that most SMEs don't have on staff, they turn to third parties to handle those duties or simply ignore regulatory obligations. The result can mean they get shut out of foreign markets, are fined spectacular fees, or get sued. The size and scope of business doesn't matter.

Outsourcing IT functions doesn't exempt companies from liability. Intermediaries are often protected from the legal ramifications of noncompliance. Big or small, if a company is out of compliance when conducting operations abroad, it can lose business very quickly not just due to foreign lawsuits but also to compensate its shareholders.[13]

## Countries Where Emotional Firewalls Hinder Internet Freedom

Some countries don't even use restrictive access laws to disrupt business. They use a technique that creates what has been coined "emotional firewalls" so that their citizens self-censor. They voluntarily avoid U.S. sites, believing they are run by spy agencies out to steal their PII. For example, when Russian troops invaded Ukraine, the rest of the world saw it as a violation of international norms. Within Russia 55 percent of its citizens applauded the country's military action because state-run media, which control practically all news outlets, feed what could reasonably be deemed propaganda to the only websites their users are able to access.

If a foreign website becomes too popular, whether it is a personal blog or a company website, it is quickly placed on a list of monitored websites that have to register with the Russian government — not to mention that Russia routinely blocks and filters websites at a whim without any real legal justification. When doing business in countries such as Russia and Turkey — which uses the same technique to imbue its citizens with emotional firewalls — there is little redress for companies. Either they adhere to imposed restrictions or avoid those markets altogether.

## World's Worst Violators of Internet Freedom

Which countries have the worst record concerning Internet freedom has actually been studied by *Freedom House* so that businesses have an idea what they will face when they expand. After conducting a multi-year survey of 65 different nations and ranking them based on their privacy and censorship laws, the survey found that more than half of those countries have seen privacy eroded and censorship laws increased over the past two years.

Surprisingly, France was one of the top three countries with the greatest decline in Internet freedom. That puts it on par with Libya and Ukraine. The nations that ranked the worst include:

- **Libya:** War has created an incredibly violent environment putting bloggers that speak out against one side or the other in danger. The cost for phone and Internet services has gone too high for most people to afford, further restricting Internet access.
- **Ukraine:** As Ukraine has battled against Russia, authorities have used violence against those speaking out in favor of the latter and prosecuted Internet users who post disparaging remarks online about the Ukrainian government.
- **France:** Since the 2015 massacre at the satirical magazine *Charlie Hebdo*'s offices by fundamentalist Muslims for publishing a cartoon of Islam's Prophet Muhammad, as well as several more bloody attacks, France has gone against traditional cultural values to prevent more terrorist assaults by restricting content and monitoring websites.
- **China**: Of all the countries in the world, the survey not surprisingly found China to be the worst when it comes to Internet freedom. Besides limiting the type of access users have, the country has over the past two years violated user privacy by instituting rules that forbid hiding their identities and jailing activists for negative posts.

## "Internet Sovereignty" in the Chinese Media (2010–2015)

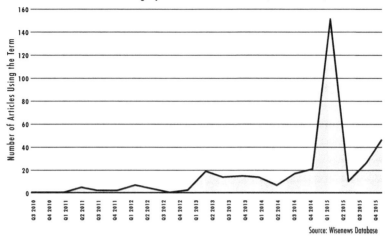

Source: Wisenews Database

- **Syria:** Activists in Syria, as the Islamic State of Iraq and Syria (ISIS) continues to battle for control of the Middle Eastern nation, are risking more than takedowns for posting unsavory comments online. Bloggers, journalists, and ordinary citizens are being killed from all sides for speaking out against atrocities.
- **Iran:** Even posting on Facebook can result in being sent to prison if people speak out against Iran's government, even though the current president has broadened access for users in that country.

Local firms, vendors, and even customers in these countries are at risk of being censored, jailed, or murdered based on the actions of foreign companies. For example, if a foreign firm posts on its news site an article unfriendly toward the Syrian government and users repost it, they could wind up dead. U.S. businesses in particular have to think long and hard whether or not to invest in areas of conflict. Believe it or not some do, but the risks can be extremely severe in some of the world's worst places for Internet freedom.

## Protecting IP and IT in Authoritarian China

Most businesses avoid hotbeds such as Syria and Iran, but the Chinese market is a lot harder to ignore as a lucrative place to expand. It is the second-largest economy in the world and growing. Online retailers have seen a more than 20 percent increase in sales every year since 2014, and China is now the largest market for online retail sales.[14]

At the same time American businesses are finding it harder and harder to operate in China's current unfriendly business climate. The U.S. Chamber of Commerce studied nearly 500 American companies doing business there. What it found is that almost 60 percent of those surveyed point to regulations that are arbitrary, opaque, and inconsistent as the biggest challenge to their businesses and a full 10 percent are planning to exit the market because of the onerous nature of Chinese Internet regulations.

Another thing the survey found is that more than 75 percent of American businesses in China feel they aren't as welcome now as they were just a couple of years ago when less than half (47 percent) felt that way. Tech companies as well as industrial suppliers feel the most unwelcome, with 44 percent in the technology sector believing that things are only going to get worse.[15]

U.S. companies don't just suspect that China is slanting the market to favor domestic companies; it is the stated policy of Xi Jinping, the country's president, to increase "Internet sovereignty" in China (see chart on previous page). What that means for tech businesses operating there is that they may be forced to share proprietary information with the government that will be used to back its own domestic versions of foreign services.

Foreign interests can't even wholly own a telecom company in China. They have to do as Apple did and link up with the country's state-run telecoms, taking a minority share only. That is, if they can get the licensing to do so, which is very unlikely. It means their competitors will be allowed to charge much less for services than they can charge and it means foreign companies and all of their online interactions will be monitored by the Chinese government — the same government that is also known to launch cyberattacks against foreign businesses!

Already those moves have resulted in losses in revenue since 2015, with 36 percent of U.S. businesses either breaking even or losing profits. A few years ago nearly three-quarters of American businesses saw a profit, but that number has dropped nearly 10 percent since then.

China isn't the only country tightening its data protections against U.S. companies, not just because of the revelations of NSA spying but also embarrassing and incriminating disclosures released in the Panama Papers. Now if foreign firms operate news sites in China, they aren't allowed to own publishing services in the country. All content of that kind must now be hosted only on Chinese servers.

When Apple denied the Chinese government its source code, even though it didn't face immediate consequences, it was the victim of a cyberattack shortly after that was likely launched by the Chinese government. There is even a law now that demands companies comply when authorities ask for assistance decrypting electronic devices. This is in the name of anti-terrorism. However, what amounts to terrorism in the eyes of the Chinese government can range from people expressing their religious views to citizens questioning government authority.

Another way China is making business life hard for foreign companies is through its incredibly slow Internet speeds. Right now there are only three exit points from servers in China to support more than 600 million users. According to one report measuring the Internet speed of all the nations in the world, China ranks 84th — the worst in Asia.[16] This is especially challenging for tech companies and cloud service providers.

There is no such thing as real time because the latency rate is so high due to the network monitoring conducted by the Great Firewall, which contributes to the inconsistency of Chinese networks. No matter what line of business they are in, American companies use social media for marketing purposes. Social media sites, though, are banned in China, and file-sharing programs and apps also struggle to function over the limited bandwidth of China's servers.

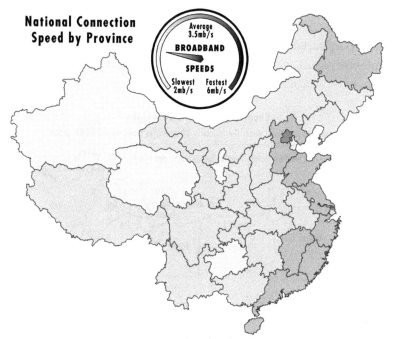

Source: Thomas Zhang, "Common Internet Challenges in China: An Overview"

Despite the many obstacles of doing business in China, nearly 70 percent of U.S. companies intend to intensify their investment dollars in the country, while over a third won't invest any more money than they already have. That is an increase of 5 percent over the past couple of years.[17] Meanwhile, the number of Chinese Internet users has been steadily growing over the past five years, leading to a potentially bigger consumer market but also even slower speeds.

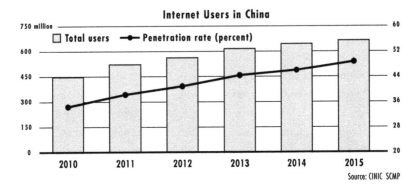

**Internet Users in China**

Source: CINIC SCMP

## War and Lack of Internet Access Hinder Business in Middle East and North Africa (MENA) Nations

For companies investing in expanding to the Middle East and North Africa (MENA) region, there are greater challenges than Internet speeds. Before even oppressive regulations, political instability and corruption are the primary concerns for foreign companies.

**Countries in the MENA Region**
According to the World Bank, the following 20 countries make up the MENA region

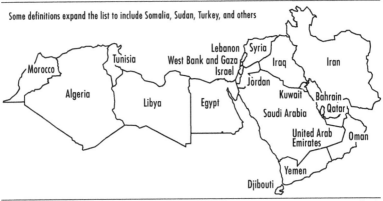

Source: World Bank

The population of the MENA region is about equivalent to that of the United States. Within those borders citizens deal with displacement, a refugee crisis, the terrorist group ISIS, and civil war throughout the region. Add to that the financial woes created by the West's waning dependence on Middle Eastern oil, which has resulted in very low oil prices, and the problems for businesses seem insurmountable.[18]

As a result, MENA governments are seeking investment to help improve their nations' economic positions, but the lack of security and political corruption prevents a lot of foreign companies from investing in MENA countries. Then there are the obvious problems most authoritarian governments present to business:

- Uncertain regulatory policy.
- Protectionist measures.
- Oppressive restrictions.
- Price manipulations.
- Network surveillance.

Notwithstanding the civil unrest, there are lucrative opportunities in some parts of the MENA region. Over the past 10 years, the number of people accessing the Internet there has soared by a staggering 2,500 percent as reported by *Risk Management*,[19] while the number of people owning mobile phones in the MENA zone has grown by nearly 20 percent — faster than any other region on the globe. That leaves possibly millions of new avenue streams for businesses willing to take the risk to invest in the MENA.

## Corruption Dissuades Business Investment in Brazil, Russia, India, and China (BRIC)

As in the MENA, foreign companies also list corruption at the top of the challenges dissuading business investment in Brazil, Russia, India, and China (BRIC). Two of the BRIC countries (Russia and China) have the greatest corruption problems, according to a Dow Jones survey.[20] U.S. companies are subject to the Foreign Corrupt Practices Act (FCPA), which prevents many businesses from investing there. Yet China still remains at the top of the list of nations viewed as preferred for more foreign investment.

**CEOs Continue to See Investment Opportunities Across BRIC**

Q: Which three countries, excluding the one in which you are based, do you consider most important for your overall growth prospects over the next 12 months?

| | |
|---|---|
| U.S. | 39% |
| China | 34% |
| Germany | 19% |
| U.K. | 11% |
| India | 9% |
| Brazil | 8% |
| Japan | 5% |
| Russia | 5% |
| Mexico | 5% |
| UAE | 5% |

Source: www.pwc.com/gx/en/ceo-survey/2016/landing-page/pwc-19th-annual-global-ceo-survey.pdf

Further complicating Internet policy for companies investing in the BRIC region are the new and emerging domestic regulations arising in each country. While some, like Germany, Mexico, and Japan, are modeling many of their regulations after global norms, there could be some rules aimed at governing domestic cyberspace that could add to the difficulties businesses face in those nations.

## Best Practices for U.S. Businesses Operating Abroad

There are ways to navigate complex waters abroad. First, businesses have to think about potential problems before expanding into difficult foreign markets. Too often Western companies begin and end with profit margins and don't consider the numerous ways foreign restrictions can eat into their bottom lines and, in fact, wind up costing huge fees for violations.

Second, companies should let their consumers and the world know when they are being forced to censor content. Although a move like that could get their websites shut down or monitored, or cause them to lose their licenses to do business in those countries, they can force those nations to handle censoring instead of putting the onus on their own companies. The American Civil Liberties Union (ACLU) suggests issuing reports publicly detailing the number of takedown or deletion requests a firm operating in an authoritarian country receives and where they are coming from.[21]

Some companies use the request review process to stretch out the time it takes to act on takedowns. If they institute policies for responding to and complying with requests but decide to create protocols that take several months to complete an investigation, they can at least delay takedowns, which will have the added effect of discouraging constant requests, since each one takes so long to investigate.

Probably the most important thing companies can do when they decide to expand business abroad is to create their own internal corporate policies based on the regulations that apply to their businesses. Working with their legal and IT departments, they can cover all their bases to get a better idea of the real cost benefit of expansion.

Finally, there are industry guidelines and international business groups such as the Global Network Initiative made up of a variety of businesses and organizations with experience working in these regions. The U.S. government is also a great source for American companies thinking about entering foreign markets that have complicated Internet regulatory policies.

# 7

## Third-Party Versus In-House IT Compliance Management

*Let's make it simple. Government control means uniformity, regulation, fees, inspection, and yes, compliance.*

— U.S. CONGRESSMAN TOM GRAVES[1]

*More and more companies are reaching out to their suppliers and contractors to work jointly on issues of sustainability, environmental responsibility, ethics, and compliance.*

— SIMON MAINWARING, *WE FIRST*[2]

*What we are seeing now is customers shifting their attention from security products like firewalls and intrusion sensors, to the policies that need to be in place, and the technologies that help them enforce policy compliance.*

— JOHN W. THOMPSON, FORMER SYMANTEC CEO AND CHAIRMAN[3]

GLOBAL INTERNET POWERHOUSES such as Facebook and YouTube can afford to spend millions of dollars to hire a team of professionals from a variety of backgrounds to help them successfully manage IT compliance. But for many businesses that lack the resources to hire a robust in-house IT staff, the avalanche of new regulations, if they are aware of them, can make the costs of doing business too much to bear.

For those companies, third-party IT management is a huge asset. A business can outsource network management to skilled experts who can help build infrastructure and secure it for a fraction of the cost of hiring in-house IT professionals who require huge salaries and good benefits. Some experts are even knowledgeable about IT regulations and how to ensure compliance.

Still, many companies are wary of turning over all their IT management to a third party. With the way technology and the regulatory environment surrounding it are changing, some businesses might have no choice but to turn to third-party service providers for assistance with IT regulatory compliance. So which is best? What are the downsides to using a third party as opposed to in-house regulatory management, and how can a reliable third-party service provider be chosen?

SMEs of all shapes and sizes have been able to build successful businesses both domestically and abroad, mainly due to the Internet but also because they can hire expert IT managers without paying for an in-house IT staff. This greatly reduces the overhead costs for companies compared to decades ago when adopting computer technology meant bringing on paid employees with high salaries and benefits, not to mention the hardware investment.

Today with very little hardware — a simple laptop and smartphone — a business can produce a money-making operation that brings in millions of dollars. Yet as IT regulations become more and more complex, as the world expands and shrinks according to politics, and governments continue to vie for supremacy in the global market, is third-party IT management the best way to go?

One of the greatest advantages of outsourcing IT management to a third party is the nimbleness of third-party IT managers. Often working for a variety of clients from a number of different industries, third-party IT service providers usually have an in-depth knowledge of every aspect of IT management, including regulatory compliance.

On the other hand, maintaining an in-house IT staff that benefits from the knowledge and expertise of a company's legal department and leadership has its own advantages. Which is better and what goes into making the decision whether or not to outsource or in-house IT?

## Change Is the Only Certainty for IT Policymakers

Today many businesses manage their IT policies on the fly as lay people. They use web-host services and web-building firms to manage the function of their business websites to take advantage of the enormous cost savings that can be had using automation, cloud computing, and wireless technology. But who is managing risk for these businesses? Who is in charge of ensuring there is an internal IT policy and that it is in full compliance with local, state, federal, and for many, international regulations?

When the constant change in the industry is the only thing business owners and IT network managers can count on anymore, scalability and speed become the two indispensable qualities of IT infrastructure. It appears that businesses are now going to have to invest at least part of their revenues into hiring either the internal staff to handle both network management and regulatory compliance or employing a third-party IT service provider.

A survey aimed at understanding the trends in regulatory compliance of cloud computing in 2015 found that the large majority of businesses invests more money in managing IT compliance.[4] The study also revealed new investments for business IT networks in:

- Risk management.
- In-house compliance officers.
- Increased network management expenditures.
- Company cultural changes to improve compliance.

In fact, among the chief challenges for businesses, bringing all stakeholders on board will be one of the toughest. That includes a shift in culture from simply trying to prepare for compliance when a review is coming up to altering the mindset of all employees toward taking an active role in enforcing compliance from top down and bottom up.

Consumers, vendors, partners, executives, and employees all have an interest in ensuring companies thrive. By changing the culture first, decision-makers are finding that internal IT protocols and policies are easier to follow and comply with when business processes reflect a commitment to staying in compliance. For instance, data necessary for SOX reviews and audits is collected throughout the year, monitored, and reported internally as part of operations so that when they actually become due a company is already prepared.

### New Regulations Are Coming Fast and Furiously

Collecting data to meet different regulatory reporting requirements isn't always easy to do and, in fact, is getting harder. New regulations from every corner of the globe and across the United States could make data collection even more difficult, which in turn will put many businesses, particularly small and midsized ones, at risk of being out of compliance. The United States alone has dozens of regulations coming online over the next while, and new financial instruments will bring into focus international monetary policies such as:

- The U.S. Foreign Corrupt Practices Act (FCPA).
- The Canadian Anti-Spam Legislation (CASL).

- The European Union's Global Basel III.
- Australia's Solvency II.
- Britain's Future of Financial Advice.

Businesses out of compliance with some EU privacy regulations could be fined tens of millions of euros and could lose their licenses to operate in EU countries. It used to be that U.S. privacy laws could be depended on to be at least as stringent as international partners; however, recent changes by EU nations make their privacy standards, in some cases, much higher than U.S. standards of privacy.

## Liability Is Shifting to Compliance Officers

Until now the Health Insurance Portability and Accountability Act (HIPAA) and Control Objectives for Information and Related Technologies (COBIT) were good general guides for businesses to meet IT compliance standards. Now, with security threats creating more distrust and a leerier consumer base, staying ahead of regulations has become an entirely separate job. Imagine missing an important EU regulation concerning data collection for an online retail website and then discovering the company is in violation and doesn't have the data required for proper reporting or has collected too much data without the consent of its consumers.

Businesses and their bottom lines could take a fatal blow they won't recover from. Network managers as well as company executives overseeing those departments could be held personally liable for breaches and noncompliance, according to over 90 percent of personal liability and compliance specialists who predict an increase in personal liability for third parties and individuals.

Many businesses mistakenly believe their third parties are responsible for data breaches that result in exposure of PII for consumers, vendors, partners, and shareholders. In reality it is the collectors of the data who are held liable, not the intermediaries. However, as the study mentioned above revealed, many in the industry almost unanimously expect that to change.[5]

## Third-Party Versus In-House IT Compliance Management — Which Is Better?

Besides increasing liability for individual compliance officers, there is a rolling back of protections for intermediaries for collecting and retaining PII. Notwithstanding the likelihood that any and all of the more than 50,000 new regulations around the globe being considered will change before they are implemented, the ability to quickly adjust to new regulations will depend on answering this question: Is third-party IT management better than in-house IT compliance management?

First of all, the business type and industry being operated in will determine how much help is needed with compliance. Take for instance payment processors such as PayPal and online banking sites, which are held to very strict regulations governing financial transactions. These businesses often employ a team of in-house compliance officers to manage regulations as they apply to all departments, including IT. Some call on their lawyers in their legal departments to decipher Internet regulations in order to meet regulatory standards. As with anything else, weighing the pros and cons is the best way to determine which IT management structure works best.

### Pros and Cons of In-House IT Compliance Management

Immediately, one pro stands out — with in-house IT compliance company officers are more in control of business operations. On the other hand, unless there are staff members with the proper expertise to be aware and have the time to stay ahead of all new threats to networks at all times, they will likely miss important updates or fail to catch network intrusions before damage is done.

In-house IT compliance also has the benefit of employees who are most familiar with specific business operations and culture. This knowledge gives them deeper insights into employee behaviors and how to craft corporate IT policy. On the other hand, there are hundreds of choices for third-party providers and even more coming online all the time. With a little due diligence, third-party providers can be found who are skilled at understanding businesses and devising tailored IT policies that work for companies.

### Pros and Cons of Third-Party IT Management

Of course, using a third party to manage IT compliance eliminates thousands of dollars in overhead costs each month. Instead of paying several regular salaries with benefits, a monthly fee can be paid to manage all IT. Some firms offer à la carte solutions that focus on which areas of IT need to be managed — regulatory compliance, for example.

Most online companies use cloud computing at one level or another to manage their data. This area alone is under the most scrutiny as new regulations are debated and implemented. Third-party IT providers are usually up-to-date with all regulations out of necessity, since they typically manage multiple clients from a wide variety of industries. Other pros include:

- More secure networks.
- Advanced IT knowledge.
- Better risk management solutions.
- Proprietary software tools.
- Constant network monitoring.
- Safer data collection and storage.
- Faster and more scalable networks.

On the downside, handing over IT compliance duties to a third party currently benefiting from intermediary liability protections could prove costly. If a third party is unaware of new regulations that affect how and for how long data can be collected and stored, the responsibility for that oversight falls on the company that hired the third party, not the intermediary. The International Data Corporation (IDC) predicts that by 2017, businesses will have spent well over $100 billion on cloud computing.

Many businesses push back, asking for more liability to rest on the shoulders of compliance officers and third-party IT managers. Findings made by numerous industry experts point to insufficient network architecture that doesn't capture requisite compliance data in real time for the majority of reporting oversights. In hiring third parties, business owners hope their monthly investments will ensure they are actually in compliance, and that if they aren't, the party responsible for creating and managing that network will be held accountable.

In the meantime, cloud computing will provide its own challenges to meet the privacy policies of different countries around the globe. Those companies that work in health care in any capacity will have to employ IT professionals on their teams to manage data collection and processing that don't violate HIPAA law.[6] Even online retailers with niche businesses could be subject to SOX and other international financial regulations when they allow their customers to pay for products or services online.

Expect most new regulations to come with systems for enforcing compliance, which means IT managers will also have to be thoroughly briefed about any new reports that must be issued both domestically and internationally, monthly, quarterly, and annually. Removing intermediary liability protections might only temporarily shift the burden of compliance. Remember, consumers really don't know or understand the inner workings of payment systems.

If there are breaches that put PII at risk, third-party providers won't be punished. Instead, the businesses that entrusted their PII to intermediaries will be disciplined. Not only will they be subject to hefty penalties and fines for noncompliance but their reputations will likely suffer, as well. Part of the appeal of third parties is their ability to provide regular audits that can alert companies to deficiencies before they cause bigger problems. Audits in turn are necessary to help businesses undergo federal Risk and Authorization Management Program (RAMP) compliance. Some of the largest tech companies model their network compliance after RAMP standards used to vet cloud providers working with U.S. government agencies.

## In-House IT Regulatory Management — Legal or IT's Job?

An accounting department is largely responsible for SOX compliance, yet many other departments are accountable for contributing their pieces to the puzzle to ensure overall compliance. So a SOX audit involves accounting, IT, and legal departments, as well as other sections of a company. There are milestones to be met for each division as they relate to financial reporting.

When it comes to IT network management, is regulatory compliance the job of the legal or IT department? That is an important question to ask because a legal team might not be aware or even able to understand all of the technical machinations behind network security and management. How then is it supposed to be depended on to assess accurately whether or not IT is in compliance with local, state, federal, and international regulations?

On the opposite side of the coin, is it fair or even reasonable to expect in-house IT professionals to be as well versed in regulations full of legalese as in-house lawyers are? On the surface, as it applies to efficiency of processes, this conflict costs businesses time and money, according to a survey done in 2015:

- At least 60 percent of businesses spent upward of three hours on regulatory compliance policy and procedures each week.
- Close to 20 percent expected that the number of hours committed to regulatory compliance would go up, with slightly more than 20 percent saying they would have to spend at least seven hours on compliance every week going forward.
- Three-quarters of those in regulatory management believe that more upper-level management officers need to be involved in IT compliance.
- Over 30 percent of businesses devote a full workday to analyzing new regulations each week.[7]

Spending that much time on regulatory compliance can eat into a company's overall productivity. No one wants a legal department to spend hours each week focusing on IT regulations when more urgent duties lie elsewhere. In the same vein, a CIO needs to be involved in big-company decisions such as expansion in order to help weigh cost benefits as they apply to network management and the feasibility of doing so.

Here is a quick rundown of the ways some businesses organize IT regulatory compliance management:

- Some businesses hire an IT expert to work within the legal department to ensure compliance.
- Some businesses send their CIOs back to school to improve their skills at monitoring and implementing internal IT policies to meet regulatory compliance standards.
- Some businesses look for software tools designed specifically to capture data needed for regulatory compliance for their specific industries.
- Some companies hire professionals to help implement customized training programs to create a compliance culture within the entire organization.

Any internal IT policy devised, whether it is in-house or with a third party, must be able to account for changing and future regulations. If new dollars have to be reinvested to update protocols every time a new regulation becomes mandatory, a lot of money and productivity will be lost. There must be constant vigilance and proactive focus on getting ahead of regulatory policy to avoid the pitfalls of noncompliance in today's volatile regulatory environment.

## Using Third-Party Providers with Caution

It might appear to SMEs that there is no other choice but to go with a third party, despite the possible risks involved. However, third-party providers must be employed with caution. Not all of them have the requisite skills needed to stay in compliance. They might not offer specific services that can be customized to individual businesses' needs. Furthermore, if third-party providers aren't vetted carefully, the companies contracting them could wind up facing criminal charges. In 2015 the Organisation for Economic Co-operation and Development (OECD) found in its 2014 Foreign Bribery Report that 75 percent of corruption cases in part involved a third party.[8]

Of those CEOs surveyed in 2015, 70 percent had seen corruption's impact on their companies lessen due to cooperation across international borders to prevent bribery and fraud. Additionally, the report found that by instituting policies that comply with regulations, companies were better able to discover corruption through self-reporting.

**How Are Foreign Bribery Cases Detected by Law Enforcement?**

| | |
|---|---|
| **31%** Self-report | **2%** Whistle-blower |
| | **2%** International organization |
| | **2%** Investigation into other offense |
| **13%** Law enforcement | **1%** Financial intelligence unit |
| | **1%** Oil-for-food |
| | **1%** Report from public |
| **13%** Mutual legal assistance | **29%** Unknown |
| **5%** Media | |

Source: OECD Foreign Bribery Report (2014)

If a third-party IT service provider is chosen to manage network compliance, there are best practices to ensure compliance is maintained:

- Third parties that are used must be able to customize their services to suit specific lines of business.
- Companies must be involved in designing IT compliance programs. All executive department heads handling electronic data must be monitored for compliance and should be involved in developing and training in their areas of IT compliance.
- Compliance procedures must be part of everyday business operations so that data needed for reporting is collected in real time.
- Third-party IT managers must be vetted for regulatory compliance, network infrastructure design, certifications, and proactive monitoring of regulatory policy.
- Regular reports on a monthly or quarterly basis must be generated so that any deficiencies early on can be detected before annual reports and audits are mandated.
- Data collection notices must be included as part of overall compliance policy for website and online transactions.

- A mechanism for requesting consent from European and Canadian users must be created to meet GDPR and PIPEDA electronic privacy requirements.

There are two more points when hiring in-house employees or using third parties for IT regulatory compliance. The skills required to manage network functionality and regulatory compliance are different. CIOs must be able to correctly interpret regulations that are jargon-heavy to prevent oversights and noncompliance. Hiring in-house might require two separate IT positions — one charged with IT regulatory compliance and another to handle infrastructure and security.

Investing in the type of software programs that can streamline compliance processes will go a long way to meet this next point: IT regulatory management must be a company-wide effort. From front desk support to public cloud storage, the information used to run a business that is sent and received online will be subject to different regulatory mandates. Staying ahead of constantly changing regulations requires the whole company to work toward that goal.

# 8

# Meeting IT Regulatory Obligations

*Small wonder that confidence languishes, for it thrives only on honesty, on honor, on the sacredness of obligations, on faithful protection, on unselfish performance; without them it cannot live.*

— FORMER U.S. PRESIDENT FRANKLIN D. ROOSEVELT[1]

*While the Census Bureau already has a legal obligation to keep people's information confidential, we all know that in an age of cyber attacks and computer hacking that ensuring people's privacy can be difficult.*

— U.S. CONGRESSMAN JEFF DUNCAN[2]

*The thing we should all be looking for are people who want to make a difference. I'm a big believer in the Silicon Valley religion of the power of markets. But I also believe in our obligation to give back, and to give back in the way we do business, to create more value than we capture for ourselves.*

— TIM O'REILLY, FOUNDER AND CEO OF O'REILLY MEDIA[3]

**E**VERYONE DEPENDS ON THEIR DATA to be kept safe and for businesses to thrive. As such IT managers are an essential part of the overall health of companies. Whether businesses employ in-house IT managers or outsource to third-party providers, when they fail to meet IT regulatory obligations, everybody suffers, from companies as a whole down to their customers and vendors. Few IT professionals have previously been counted on to have legal expertise as well as technological expertise, but that is exactly what is required going forward.

Industry to industry there are different regulatory obligations affecting the way business is conducted. When IT professionals are hired, it is imperative that consideration be given to how well versed they are in IT regulations as well as to their ability to build and protect network infrastructure. The initial step to meeting IT regulatory obligations is to make smart hires in the first place.

That could mean choosing a qualified third party or recruiting IT experts with the relevant skills to manage Internet operations. As discussed in previous chapters, fines in some countries can total tens of millions of dollars if a company is found out of compliance. What are the best practices to ensure regulatory compliance and how can a company be certain that it is meeting its obligations?

Although many business executives might see regulations as largely a hindrance, the truth is they often help improve a business. Such is the case with Internet regulations and protections. Granted, nearly every regulation falls short of ideal protections, and as has been pointed out frequently in this book, they can be conflicting, contradictory, and flat-out wrongheaded.

Nevertheless, regardless of personal feelings concerning regulations that companies face, they can't be avoided and compliance is crucial to business success. Whether required to institute more stringent measures to guard private and personal data or prevented from storing data outside a home country's borders, violations cost a business money, productivity, freedom to operate, and brand reputation.

To prevent that, network managers must be prepared for the many levels of regulatory obligations that need to be covered. Regulations that include all types of companies will have an effect on several IT-related business functions, including:

- Data collection and storage.
- Network security.
- Threat and compliance analysis.
- Network infrastructure.
- Electronic financial reporting.
- Network monitoring.
- Network access.
- Encryption and authentication.

A thorough understanding of U.S. policy pertaining to a specific business helps to meet at least half of possible regulatory obligations. In fact, some regulations, though they don't exclusively apply to any particular industry, satisfy at least a majority of a firm's domestic obligations. Following those measures can give guidance on how to craft certain company IT policies.

## Which Regulatory Obligations Should Apply to a Business?

Trying to detail exactly every regulation that a company will have to deal with by industry type isn't very helpful. There are too many exceptions to some of these rules, and depending on what city, state, or country a firm operates in, its regulatory obligations will vary. For the sake of guidance, what follows are four business types that will likely have to deal with the strictest and more numerous IT regulations and how U.S. law can serve to ensure compliance.[4]

### Health-Care Industries

The HIPAA governs electronic communications and data collection for any business operating in the health-care industry. That includes hospitals, clinics, medical research facilities, medical device manufacturers, pharmacies, medical record billing and coding, medical insurers, et cetera. One study sought to identify overlapping and conflicting regulations as they apply to a variety of businesses under different U.S. electronic regulations. What was discovered is that there are several mandates in the law that only apply to certain IT processes:

- **Security Management:** The right permissions must be granted for reviewers and those who need access to electronic protected health information (ePHI) using software. No infrastructure or platform specifications are necessary.
- **Security Officers:** A designated individual responsible for ensuring network security must be available to create and implement security protocols and policies. There are no platform or infrastructure requirements.
- **Limited Access:** Access to certain electronic health records at both the software and platform levels must be restricted. There is no infrastructure requirement.
- **Segmenting Networks:** Access controls at the infrastructure level are necessary to prevent individual employees from acquiring protected health information. All three levels must include these protections — software, platform, and infrastructure.
- **Auditing and Record-Keeping:** Mechanisms must be created to record

any activity whether authorized or unauthorized in which health PII was accessed. Compliance reporting must be done at all three levels — software, platform, and infrastructure.

## Online Retailers

Online retailers come in all sizes. Artists sell paintings worth thousands of dollars through online galleries and auctions. Also, of course, there are big-name retail chains such as Home Depot and Macy's that allow purchases to be made online. Practically every business that provides a service or a good has an online retail component. In order to stay in compliance, here are some regulations that apply to businesses handling online purchases:

- **Firewall Protection:** Online retailers have to install firewalls designed to keep customer credit card information safe. Protections like those are required at the software, platform, and infrastructure levels.
- **Password Protection:** There are mandates in the PCI DSS regulation that dictate system defaults for passwords and other security features. Protocols must be established for compliance at both the software and platform levels but not at the infrastructure level.
- **Data Storage:** Mandates regulating how customer credit card data is stored must be put in place at both the platform and software levels only.
- **Encryption Requirements:** Any time customer PII is sent and received online, particularly over public networks, it has to be encrypted at the software and platform levels.
- **Anti-Virus Protection:** Company CIOs must maintain sufficient anti-virus software that is kept up-to-date at the software and platform levels.
- **Access Restrictions:** At all levels access to user data must be restricted on a need-to-know basis.

Just as in the health-care industry, online retailers have to issue reports detailing their compliance and the policies that are in place. There are many more IT regulations governing online transactions. The most important thing to consider is privacy protections, since these are the most sweeping regulatory changes taking place.

## Money Managers

No longer are banks the only money managers. Payments are made online using PayPal, Google Wallet, bitcoins, and more. What defines a money manager will continue to change as cloud computing makes instant financial transactions easier. Banks, investment firms, payment processors, et cetera, will butt up against several laws governing how financial data electronically sent and received is secured. The FISMA is the best guide for U.S. businesses devising IT security policies for online transactions. It covers most regulations, including PCI DSS, HIPAA, and ISO regulations, but it won't suffice for privacy protection regulations.

### Cloud Service Providers

Perhaps cloud service providers have the most to worry about when it comes to meeting the IT regulatory obligations of their clients. Because the cloud is ubiquitous and service providers aren't limited by physical location, data requirements and privacy restrictions could present an enormous challenge for network managers. Moreover, laws such as the GDPR that mandate the creation of new officers within a company to be responsible for compliance must also be noted and adhered to. Currently, the EUDPD contains rules that require businesses to encrypt and make user data anonymous to protect PII. As data breaches and cybercrimes continue to rise, expect these types of regulations to get even tighter for cloud service providers.

## Managing Conflicting and Overlapping Regulations

There isn't much that can be done as a business to cure the overlaps in regulations, but hiring IT professionals with expert knowledge of network architecture is something that can help. With a solid network design that takes into consideration regulatory policy, software protocols can be implemented to collect data according to standards and store it. CIOs can then work with other departments to identify the types of data that must be accounted for in designing network architecture so that the guesswork is taken out of compliance and automation ensures it.

Third-party providers are often skilled at creating network architectures that can account for patterns in regulations, and some can even construct a custom software program to capture the data needed to meet regulatory obligations.

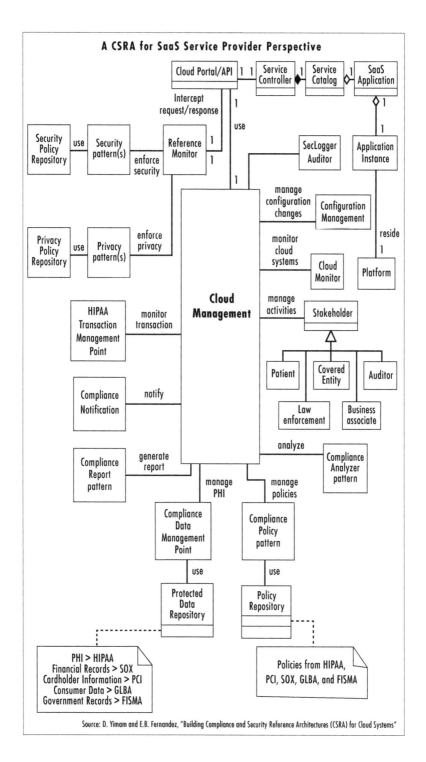

A CSRA for SaaS Service Provider Perspective

Source: D. Yimam and E.B. Fernandez, "Building Compliance and Security Reference Architectures (CSRA) for Cloud Systems"

Unless a CIO is able to analyze and build network security and privacy protections into system architecture in a way that makes sense and meets compliance, a company is likely to miss important reporting requirements. Or it could end up wasting considerable hours in productivity every week trying to capture that information on its own instead of using automation to eliminate redundancies and verify that compliance hurdles are being met.

With network detail like that, mandates to encrypt and make anonymous, data localization requirements, and reporting mandates can be achieved. All that will be necessary to implement protocols to request consent to collect private information from European consumers, merely to name one reason to figure out how to manage conflicting regulations.

## Developing Internal IT Protocols to Ensure Compliance

Unfortunately, there are few industry standards that break down regulations that conflict and overlap so that businesses have a known model to follow to ensure compliance. Instead, each business is responsible for hiring and/or developing the talent and skills necessary to define IT protocols with precision. When developing internal IT protocols, there are several standard steps that will help to achieve compliance with regulations:

1. Know the regulations specific to wherever the business operates.
2. Detail the mandates that apply to business operations, including network mapping.
3. Find out the areas of business responsible for meeting these mandates and identify a compliance officer.
4. Conduct initial reviews as measuring sticks through compliance testing.
5. Analyze results to improve processes for more accurate and efficient data capture.
6. Reassess and evaluate through regular program review and compliance testing.

Where a CIO or third-party IT provider comes in is to build the type of network architecture that can automate processes to efficiently verify and validate compliance. Importantly, a CIO must test and retest those processes for flexibility, accuracy, reliability, and functionality, among other things. Overarching all this data capture is network security that doesn't conflict with compliance protocols.

## Planning Internet Security for Future Global Businesses

Using a third party ensures the same systems and platforms are used to operate security protocols as the ones that protect data collection and storage. Consistency is rule number one in developing the proper sort of network architecture that can help meet regulatory obligations. Businesses are especially focused on preventing cyberattacks more than building reference architecture (RA) models for regulatory compliance. There is a logical reason for that — most recent cyberattacks have been aimed at businesses.[5]

The problem is that online criminals are changing and branching out. They are attacking consumers, smartphones, mobile devices, big banks, movie studios, and government officials. There is practically no limit to the ways in which network intrusions are aimed at businesses. Sometimes it is simply because a network isn't strong enough.

Evidence shows that the bulk of successful cyber sweeps occur because systems are vulnerable more than the specific cache of data being targeted. Said another way, if a hacker can siphon off money from a bank account without being noticing because the network protection is so weak, it is more cost-feasible than attempting to hack into a major multinational bank's financial system.

In fact, increasing attacks on health-care facilities and government records reveal that criminals are more interested in stealing data that can be used to pilfer money on a larger scale rather than big scores where the risks of getting caught are higher. That is leading businesses to beef up their network security, hoping to make the effort to infiltrate those systems much harder and therefore less worthwhile for hackers.

## Geopolitical Realities Will Affect Future IT Regulatory Obligations

Part of what keeps IT regulatory policy in a state of constant flux is the geopolitical realities that have always and will continue to affect the technological landscape. One of the major reasons why the TPP largely left international cybersecurity policy untouched was because there was no certainty or uniformity of ideas for reducing online criminality.

As businesses confront regulations coming down on every front, consumers expect faster access with the comfort of knowing that their information is safe. Internal IT policy often comes from the top down with marketing and business objectives mainly in mind. However, going forward,

IT policy will increasingly have to align with regulatory obligations as well as with mandates for data security.

Additionally, as privacy laws and other protectionist measures spread throughout the globe, more authoritarian policies proliferate, albeit on a much smaller scale. For instance, China in the name of national security has already begun instituting stringent data localization laws that could have a considerable impact on trade between China and the United States.

On the other hand, Russia is openly and secretly using nation-to-nation and nation-to-business cyberattacks to further political gain and disrupt commercial rivals. The United States has also used online deterrence as part of military operations abroad — the largest and most noted being the attack on the Iranian centrifuges that completely destroyed Iran's uranium-enrichment program.

## Costs of Network Security Will Only Rise

While costs for hiring IT experts capable of deciphering national and international IT regulations are inevitable, so are escalating expenses for network security. One survey predicts the price of cybercrime to businesses around the world will reach more than $6 trillion by 2021.[6] Costs go beyond simply repairing networks after security breaches. Businesses doing business online will have to secure their data against:

- Data theft.
- Embezzlement.
- Disruptive attacks.
- Fraud.
- IP theft.
- Ransomware attacks.

Naturally, online thieves are also capable of stealing money directly from business accounts with a few bits of corporate or individual information. It might be that the focus on deterring cybercrime has caused businesses to overlook the impact that so many regulations will have on the way information is kept and shared. This could have the effect of stifling the technological innovation and creativity that brought forth the Idea Economy.

In an economy where information is as valuable as money itself, any moves that limit information sharing could have a ripple effect on global trade policy. Even now the IoT is only in its infancy relative to cloud and mobile technology and yet presents the potential for more complicated regulatory policy as well as new opportunities for cybercrime to flourish. According to one statistic, businesses will have to spend between 10 and 15 percent of their annual IT budgets on cybercrime deterrence going forward.[7]

As much money as is being spent in network security, the bulk will be devoted to building data centers where data localization presents a challenge, creating systems that connect more M2M and wireless devices and providing platform and infrastructure services to account for security and data storage.

## Some Outsourced IT Providers Are Diversifying and Growing

Outsourcing network security is predicted to outpace all other segments of the IT market. That said, there are new third-party providers springing up to offer more niche IT security services that account for regulatory obligations by industry, including:

- Systems integration specialists.
- Mobile security providers.
- IT services for law firms.
- Accounting IT providers.
- Outsourced online retail IT.
- Third-party human resource management.

There are third-party providers that offer network security and architecture design specifically for lawyers or accountants. Their role will increasingly combine industry knowledge with regulatory standards for capturing and reporting electronic information.

Another area where there is expected growth in the outsourced IT industry is for individual consumers. Standard firewalls and anti-virus protections have left many users vulnerable to cyberattacks and data breaches. Largely due to user negligence, this problem is only going to get bigger as hackers are now targeting mobile users who are even more careless with Internet security on their mobile devices.[8] Expect new third-party providers to come online offering security services for individuals.

## New Technologies Will Affect Regulatory Policy

Just as hackers seek out ways to infect millions of mobile devices with ransomware and other data theft tools, new technologies developing around cloud computing, the IoT, and M2M technology will further affect regulatory policy.

Take for example the tidal shift among millennials from standard broadband TV access to online viewing using 4G, and soon, 5G technology. Will regulators bring Internet technology under the umbrella of telecoms? How will the infrastructure required to support these new technologies be regulated?[9]

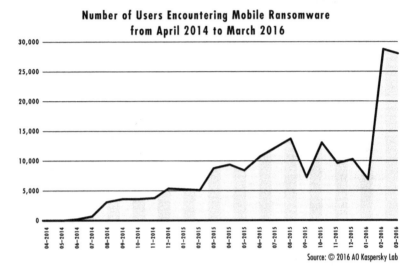

**Number of Users Encountering Mobile Ransomware from April 2014 to March 2016**

Source: © 2016 AO Kaspersky Lab

Currently, there is already enormous pushback in light of the federal court decision upholding the FCC ruling that Internet access is a public utility. Will wireless technology have a similar fight on the horizon as more and more people, particularly in the United States, watch TV online on their mobile devices? Think of the regulatory hurdles that will have to be overcome to provide virtual assistance services in Europe in the face of data localization laws or the feasibility of Amazon delivering packages using drones. Regulators have struggled for several years to design policies that account for cloud computing and wireless. Expect new and emerging technologies to add new wrinkles to IT regulatory obligations.

## Accounting for the Internet of Things (IoT) in Global Regulations

Today houses are being built with smart technology that allows homeowners to turn heat up or down from their mobile devices or remotely switch on outdoor lights and more. The Internet of Things (IoT) appears to be a game changer on multiple fronts. Individually, it will mean a more technology-driven existence in which everything from cars, to homes, to pets are linked to the Internet.

On the macro-scale, M2M technology and the IoT are going to have regulatory implications for militaries, business operations, public utilities, and payment systems. Around the globe the IoT alone is expected to generate more than $4.5 trillion over the next six years.[10]

One way that businesses can meet regulatory obligations as they apply to the IoT is to begin testing the ways in which companies can benefit from the IoT and what regulations will affect it. Keep in mind that in addition to accounting for the feasibility of using the IoT in day-to-day operations the cost benefits must be weighed as they pertain to the regulatory standards required to utilize certain technologies.

Again, in the European Union, simple access to e-mail addresses and other identifying information used in everyday online transactions in the United States could be deemed in violation for those customers. Are the pluses countered by the costs of compliance? Factoring in regulatory expenses along with the benefits of adopting new technologies will go a long way to help devise an appropriate internal IT policy that accounts for the IoT.

## The Role of Distributed Ledger Technology in Future E-Commerce

Perhaps one of the most daunting challenges in e-commerce of the future is deciding the role of distributed ledger technology (DLT) and how to regulate it. Four years ago the International Organization of Securities Commissions (IOSC) developed rules governing international payments in an attempt to account for new payment systems. These principles, known as the Principles for Financial Market Infrastructures (PFMIs), are now being applied to a new and growing type of payment system: DLT.[11]

DLT is the same technology used by bitcoins, the online currency exchange that first got its start as an online gambling payment tool. Bitcoins have since gone from a niche to being seriously discussed by regulators as part of the global financial market infrastructure. However, the PFMI standards are industry-regulated, and there is no way to enforce compliance. So, as DLT has gained in popularity, regulators are now forced to define its role in the global marketplace.

A serious problem DLT faces is that the technology is still not viable as an underpinning payment system in the global financial system. Bitcoins themselves have been targeted several times by hackers with success. Yet the idea of creating payment systems that can be used in countries where citizens don't have ready access to bank accounts or credit cards is an intriguing one.

Unfortunately for proponents of DLT, not only is the functional technology years away but so is any sense of regulatory uniformity. This technology will have to be regulated by the Federal Reserve, the Commodity Futures Trading Commission (CFTC), the Securities and Exchange Commission (SEC), and local and state regulators. Add in the challenge of cross-border data flow restrictions and DLT is facing numerous hurdles before it becomes as ubiquitous as other online payment technologies. However, the U.S. government is currently studying what it defines as "fintech" through the Federal Reserve to proactively determine its applications and how it can be properly regulated.[12]

## Steps to Meet IT Compliance Obligations Successfully

While there is no one-size-fits-all solution to the regulatory challenges businesses will encounter, there are steps that can be taken now that will help meet IT compliance obligations successfully. These steps involve an overarching attitude and disposition toward regulations that will make implementation much easier and awareness constant:

- Think of compliance as a team effort and a shared responsibility from the CEO down to part-time staff.
- Compliance should be built into the network architecture so that much of the required data capture is automated.
- Carve out a specific slice of the IT budget for regulatory compliance instead of lumping all IT into one basket.
- Fully vet third-party providers and look for those with industry specialties.
- Institute new protocols now in order to comply with privacy laws that might soon affect the way user data is stored.

Regulatory compliance can no longer be an afterthought. It has to be part of the overall network design and implementation. Frequent testing and updating of compliance protocols are going to be part of the everyday duties of CIOs from now on.

# 9

# Is a Uniform Global IT Strategy Possible?

*Every giant leap for mankind resulting from a technological advance requires a commensurate step in the opposite direction — a counterweight to ground us in humanity.*

— ALEX MORRITT, AUTHOR[1]

*Globalism began as a vision of a world with free trade, shared prosperity, and open borders. These are good, even noble things to aim for.*

— DEEPAK CHOPRA, NEW AGE AUTHOR[2]

HERE IS A RADICAL IDEA: maybe a global IT strategy isn't even necessary to keep the Internet free and unfettered. That is one of the ideas being circulated among thought leaders attempting to figure out ways to create uniformity for global IT policy. Any global strategy seems to be dead on arrival despite the obvious dangers to global e-commerce presented by the lack of uniformity.

At this point all options must be considered. Certainly, the current lawlessness of cyberspace where online criminality flourishes and threatens businesses, individuals, and governments everywhere is untenable. Could a solution be devised that the majority of nations can get behind?

Donald Trump is now the president of the United States. In response, protests across the country both for and against him have illustrated just how fragile the ties that bind the geopolitical reality of today are and how quickly it can all change.

Over the course of this book, many laws have been examined as well as their impact on businesses around the globe. Yet, as has been stated repeatedly, the only thing to expect in the technological landscape of today is constant change. With that change are new geopolitical realities as nations and businesses compete for space and dominance in the global market.

Former President Barack Obama over the previous eight years took a leadership role in pushing a more cooperative global strategy that sought uniformity and fairness in trade and commerce. Political expert Ian Bremmer posited in an article produced just one day after Trump's election that based on the tone and rhetoric the new president pushed throughout his two-year campaign, a shrinking and less global alignment of policy and trade with countries around the world seemed likely in the future.[3]

Instead of a global strategy, what could ensue is a fragmenting global trade environment that would result in a more polarized world, leaving room for competitor nations such as China and Russia to exert more power of their own in the global space. What does this all mean for global policy over the next few years? What can businesses do to prepare for whatever eventualities might occur around global e-commerce and trade?

## The Future Will Bring More Technological Interconnectedness

Regardless of geopolitics, what is evident by the trends in technological advances over the past few years is that the future promises to be more connected. There will be more devices connected across the globe and along Internet connections that are irrespective of national boundaries. The technology is there. What isn't as certain is whether or not the global regulatory environment will be a help or hindrance to these advances.

Take for example DLTs and new real-time payment processors. Inherent to the success of such tools is the ability to share information across borders along the Internet. The speed of transactions and the efficient settling of accounts are only possible with unfettered data flows between systems that span the globe. In the same way that outsourced IT is allowing small and midsized businesses to start up without huge capital investments by slashing overhead costs, DLT is predicted to similarly eliminate much of the costs associated with money transfers and payment transactions online.

At the same time the potential for fraud schemes that could put billions at risk of identity and data theft is incalculable. The types of regulations that would have to be in place domestically and internationally for online currency that isn't tied to any real monies to be as secured as transactions backed by traditional banks would be hefty and would have to carry precipitous fines and close oversight. The means to achieve this level of global uniformity is merely theoretical at this point, but a future built off DLT will need strong security at the architectural level to prevent data theft — the kind of global Internet security that today doesn't exist.

## Uniformity Requires Broader Global Internet Access

> The current path of globalisation demands a course correction. In the years and decades ahead, our countries have to make sure that the benefits of an integrated global economy are more broadly shared by more people, and that the negative impacts are squarely addressed.
>
> — FORMER U.S. PRESIDENT BARACK OBAMA[4]

Uniformity would also help to counteract much of the imbalance created over the past two decades as Internet access became concentrated in nations already advanced. In fact, in the entire world, the countries with broad Internet access are limited to just 20 different countries in the developed world.[5] The vast majority of those without Internet access live in remote rural areas where poverty is extensive and the population is aged.

Businesses aren't incentivized to invest in broad Internet access in these places without a financial benefit. However, future innovators are finding new areas to explore by expanding Internet access in remoter areas. As the potential for global uniformity fractures, it is possible there will be broader access delineated by regional blocs.

Nations with similar values tend to flock together. Those countries that tolerate laws that infringe upon individual freedoms and privacy online create closed blocs that allow a limited group of partners to trade with one another. Similar to the TPP trade bloc, there would be different regional trade blocs that could lock out other nations.

This could limit global e-commerce and result in more protectionism. Or it could be the only way to keep cross-border data flows going, albeit in much more limited ways and areas of the globe. It could also have the negative consequence of leaving hundreds of millions, billions of global citizens barred from the opportunities created by increasing global wealth as a result of broader Internet access.

## Coordinated Global Information Sharing Can Help

*Information technology has been one of the leading drivers of globalization, and it may also become one of its major victims.*

— EVGENY MOROZOV, AUTHOR[6]

Pillars of any uniform global IT strategy are known, and global information sharing is chief among them. In every manner, the Internet is at its essence an information-sharing tool. It has grown to facilitate e-commerce and online transactions, but at its core it is an exchange of information. For any global strategy to work, regulations, internal protocols, and industry best practices have to encourage global information sharing.

However, in a climate where cybercrimes and data theft are at an all-time high, the instinct for businesses is the same for governments — to limit sharing and restrict access. These are valid principles for Internet security, but they stand in direct opposition to the necessities of commercial enterprises dependent on a less restrictive global Internet environment to thrive. Yet necessity has caused even the U.S. Energy Department to devise ways to share information with partners to better protect the country's infrastructure.

## Concerted Internet Security Strategies Can Help Combat Cybercrime

*The guardians of your company's cyber security should be encouraged to network within the industry to swap information on the latest hacker tricks and most effective defenses.*

— NINA EASTON, JOURNALIST[7]

What is also known is that to thwart the growing number of cybercrimes against businesses in every part of the world there has to be coordination among international partners. The more concerted the security apparatus, the more effective it is at frustrating criminals. Right now there is no real international body with enforcement powers to police cybercrime on a global scale. What is required is a concerted effort that nations can agree to that gives enforcement authority to all nations collectively.

Therein lies the problem — each nation has its own self-interest in mind and some have carried out a number of high-profile cyberattacks. Multiply that problem with companies competing in the same way against one another both domestically and abroad. The problem of getting all parties involved in global information sharing can be seen in the lack of a credible authority to enforce global security mandates.

Meanwhile, as of 2015, nearly 80 percent of all small businesses were unprepared for a cyberattack despite the fact that nearly two-thirds of those same businesses had already experienced a security breach in their networks. Overall, during the past five decades, cybercrimes have grown by 144 percent while businesses large and small have been targeted successfully by hackers in increasingly higher-profile attacks.

Recently, online criminals have begun forgoing attempts to attack military-grade systems such as those at the Pentagon or the National Security Agency in exchange for individual attacks against private contractors, soldiers, and diplomats with access to sensitive military information. Research facilities and businesses working in the tech industry are also high-profile targets for online thieves. Coincidentally, these entities are among the organizations most dependent on broad Internet access and global information security. The need for better Internet security will have to be lobbied for by these groups or else future efforts at a global online security strategy will continue to be stalled.

## Rising Number of Nation-State Hacks Prevents Cooperation

*An element of virtually every national security threat and crime problem the FBI faces is cyber-based or facilitated. We face sophisticated cyber threats from state-sponsored hackers, hackers for hire, organized cyber syndicates, and terrorists.*
— JAMES B. COMEY, FORMER DIRECTOR OF THE
FEDERAL BUREAU OF INVESTIGATION[8]

A surprising statistic to everyone outside law enforcement is that nation-state cyberattacks have increased dramatically. In a 2015 survey, PricewaterhouseCoopers respondents said that 86 percent of cyberattacks were backed by nation-states.[9] The same survey found that the cost to businesses grew by nearly 35 percent on average annually, going from a loss of $3 million to businesses to over $20 million in three years on average.

Identifying nation-state actors is only part of the problem. Calling them out can have enormous repercussions politically. Backlash could come from nations that deny responsibility, as is often the case when the United States accuses China or Russia of hacking into American systems, or it can come from people as was the case with the Edward Snowden leaks. In fact, approximately 50 percent of cyberattacks against governments and big corporations are committed by hacktivists rather than online thieves.

Because of this, any consensus on how to prevent such attacks will inevitably catch a few nations in the crosshairs of international Internet security regulations. For global security regulations to work there has to be agreement by the majority of nations. As nation-state attacks continue to increase, the chances of finding agreement on a set of security regulations and even how to enforce them are slim.

## Creating the Global Legal Framework to Encourage E-Commerce

Business works on incentive. If an opportunity will result in higher net profits, it is at least worth considering for most heads of companies. Making the argument that there needs to be a global legal framework that encourages e-commerce rather than inhibits it begins with making the incentives clear:

- Costs of cybercrimes to businesses are going up.
- Global e-commerce accounts for approximately 3 percent of GDP.
- Nations with open global markets generate more wealth.
- Majority of global commerce transpires online.

Moreover, consumers and partners want to work with companies that have a global reach. Challenges to strategies that aim to unify global IT regulations rest on businesses' need to build confidence in its users and consumers. Some of the commonsense security measures being proposed have been stymied because businesses and nations want the freedom to manage their own security and risk.

When large breaches happen, it shakes consumer confidence and leaves businesses vulnerable. Global regulations are viewed as being incapable of accounting for the many nuances and exceptions that affect necessary security measures from nation to nation and industry to industry. Plus some nations limit user access for purposes of monitoring or controlling their citizens in the name of security. Either way, finding conformity on global Internet security is still a long way off.

Furthermore, at the same time that nations are beginning to institute cross-border data restrictions, there is an even greater need for more freedom of data flow to facilitate new technologies. Just think of the types of data M2M technology will require for devices to function without borders consistently.

Countries enacting restrictive access laws will either be cut out of certain markets or businesses will have to cater their online services to accommodate those restrictions.

## Areas Where Change Can Be Made Now

According to the United Nations World Economic Forum, the United States is doing cybersecurity right, ranking at the top of all nations as the country with the most secure Internet. Because of that, the United States has been called upon to contribute to discussions focusing on global security regulations that could counteract cyberattacks. The World Trade Organization is also working with member nations to work on a consensus that will support free digital trade in the face of protectionist measures being enacted worldwide.

Multinational trade agreements will further enhance protections against cybercrime in the absence of a uniform global policy. Issues surrounding third-party liability and data localization can be balanced through trade agreements regardless of whether or not there is global consensus on Internet security regulations.

Still, there is the novel idea mentioned at the beginning of this chapter that few commentators have given real weight to in political discussions about ways to improve global e-commerce while increasing privacy and security. What if there is no need for a uniform global strategy?

Some could argue that it is the rapid spread of globalization that has resulted in more disparity.[10] While it is true that wealthy nations have seen enormous wealth and GDP growth due to the Internet, poorer countries have seen very little improvement.

Without the fundamentals of democracy to govern Internet access, there is too great a potential for it to be used for nefarious government reasons, as has been done. In some areas of the world in the BRIC and MENA nations, instead of Internet access resulting in greater shared prosperity, globalization has created a new means for despotic governments to pursue targeted crackdowns against dissidents and social activism.

In addition, the likelihood is practically nil for authoritarian governments to agree to global norms that respect individual privacy rights and freedom of expression in the manner that U.S. and EU laws do. Almost 40 years ago a Nobel Prize winner hypothesized at the beginning of the tech revolution that the idea of unfettered global trade was unrealistic and that the best possible arrangement geopolitically would be to build trade alliances within regional groups with shared political, social, and economic values.

Of course, that would run counter to the altruistic values long held by democratic nations that support freedom for all citizens around the globe. In a world economy in which only free people have access to the free and unfettered Internet, the problems of disparity and imbalance would certainly only deepen distrust and disharmony among nations.

## Will America Close Its Doors?

In conclusion it is hard not to circle back to what former Utah Governor Jon Huntsman, Jr., said about what happens when the planet's leading democracy closes its doors to business. When that occurs, the rest of the world will close its doors, too. Global reaction among U.S. allies to the election of Donald Trump has been cautious at best.

After a vitriolic two-year campaign, the least likely candidate won the 2016 U.S. presidential election, even though his challenger, Hillary Clinton, received almost three million more popular votes than Trump did. Granted, this election had the lowest voter turnout in a presidential election since 1996, which would also indicate that Trump lacks a real mandate. Despite that, early moves made during the transition have nations around the world poring over the sentiments expressed during those two years. Most concluded that the 2016 election could signal a closing of American doors to the progressive future of global e-commerce that the United States has always embraced.

One of the best-known points of international contention is in the metaphorical implications of an actual wall designed to physically separate the United States from Mexico. Anti-immigrant sentiment has been high since Trump's nomination to the Republican ticket, evoking a variety of responses from Latin American nations around the globe.[11]

In Colombia the nation's well-known cartoonist, Vladimir Flórez, is quoted as saying: "This threat called Trump is a product of American society; a nightmarish mutation of the American dream." Venezuelan leaders who were also targeted by Trump for being far left have warned Trump to respect "nonintervention in internal issues and to the right of development and peace."

Thanks to Trump's rhetoric during the election campaign, Latin American nations weren't the only ones taken aback in light of his victory. When it comes to trade generally, Trump has put forward the idea that America should back out of NAFTA, which would have reverberative effects on trade with Canada and Mexico.

In Poland the election of Trump, along with Britain's decision to exit the

European Union, caused Donald Tusk, the president of the European Union Council and a former Polish prime minister, to state on the record that "The events of the last months and days should be treated as a warning sign for all who believe in liberal democracy." In Belgium the alarm was equally stark, with one of that country's former prime ministers warning that "Donald Trump has declared several times that our priorities are not his."

Even the former secretary-general of the United Nations, Ban Ki-moon, pointed to America's role in the world in his comments following Trump's election. He focused on America's inclusiveness in the face of an extremely divisive campaign, saying that it is worth "recalling and reaffirming that the unity in diversity of the United States is one of the country's greatest strengths."

French President François Hollande got to the heart of the matter when he questioned what Trump's election would mean for deals that had already been struck in the world on climate and nuclear disarmament, to name a couple. After years of sanctions, President Obama's harsh policy to bring Iran to the negotiating table to end its nuclear program finally paid off. At the beginning of 2016, Iran finally agreed to end its nuclear proliferation in exchange for relief from U.S. and world sanctions — an agreement Trump wants to abandon, calling it "the worst deal ever."

Syrians in the middle of a civil war in which the United States provides air support to Iraqi and other resistance forces expressed real concern about Trump's rhetoric, adding, "Here is a man who is openly saying that he is going to defer to Russians on Syria. This is a clear victory for the Assad regime." Syrian President Bashar al-Assad was pressured and explicitly called upon to step down by former President Obama as well as by other world leaders. On top of that, Trump has riled many Muslims with his anti-Islamic rhetoric, not to mention his attempts at invoking a temporary ban of immigrants and refugees from six majority-Muslim nations.

Even in Asia where the United States has made enormous strides pushing the TPP and other alliances among Pacific nations, Trump has caused concern. Japan and South Korea are worried regarding Trump's language about cutting back military protection in their waters. One Japanese professor in response said that "if he carries out such a policy, China will be much more authoritative and aggressive in the Pacific."

*Here is something to think about. How will IT regulatory compliance be managed for businesses if the United States closes its doors?*

With all the changes happening in the world now, how will IT regulatory compliance be managed? The election of a new U.S. president with a vision in stark contrast to the one the United States has embraced over the past few decades heralds unexpected changes on the horizon — ones that have many world nations, including U.S. allies, anxious about the stability and continued cooperation of international Internet security and freedom.

What does it mean for the leading democracy and superpower in the world to rebuff old alliances and build ties with historical adversaries whose policies align more with authoritarian governments? What does that mean for businesses on a local level within the United States where states are enacting these types of protectionist laws?

Just as in self-defense, awareness of surroundings is the key. Being aware of the IT regulatory landscape of today and beyond is crucial. Knowing what to do from a business standpoint and how feasible it is will require new skills from IT management. How computer networks are built has to take center stage for all operations.

New start-ups, small and midsized businesses, and new entrepreneurs are now more important than ever to be successful in the global marketplace. To do all the things a company envisions for 2017 and beyond will take a smart and nimble network that can keep up with the times.

Staying in compliance with sometimes wildly different Internet privacy and security policies is now part of a network manager's job. The key is working together as a team, with all executives supporting their company's IT efforts, keeping everyone involved, and doing their part to protect the company and prepare it for whatever is to come.

# Notes

## Chapter 1: The Business Cost of Internet Freedom

1. Eric Schmidt, the former CEO (2001–11) of Google, said this in a speech he gave at the JavaOne Conference in April 1997 in San Francisco when he was the newly hired CEO of Novell.
2. David P. Fidler, "Hacking the Wealth of Nations: Managing Markets Amid Malware." *Turkish Policy Quarterly* 14, no. 2 (Summer 2015). Accessed at http://turkishpolicy.com/article/756/hacking-the-wealth-of-nations-managing-markets-amid-malware-summer-2015, July 24, 2017.
3. Joshua P. Meltzer, *Maximizing the Opportunities of the Internet for International Trade* (Geneva: International Centre for Trade and Sustainable Development [ICTSD], World Economic Forum, 2016). Accessed at www3.weforum.org/docs/E15/WEF_Digital_Trade_report_2015_1401.pdf, July 24, 2017.
4. Ibid.
5. Ibid.
6. Ibid.
7. Susan Ariel Aaronson, "Digital Trade Rules and Digital Protectionism" (2016). Accessed at www2.itif.org/2016-trade-rules-digital-protectionism.pdf, July 24, 2017.
8. Daphne Keller, "The Final Draft of Europe's 'Right to Be Forgotten' Law, The Center for Internet and Society, Stanford Law School, December 17, 2015. Accessed at http://cyberlaw.stanford.edu/blog/2015/12/final-draft-europes-right-be-forgotten-law, July 24, 2017.
9. Meltzer, *Maximizing the Opportunities of the Internet for International Trade.*

## Chapter 2: Breaking Down the Trans-Pacific Partnership (TPP)

1. Brett M. Decker, "5 Questions with Rep. Ralph Hall," *Washington Times*, June 26, 2012.
2. Michael Badnarik, *BrainyQuote.com*. Accessed at www.brainyquote.com/quotes/quotes/m/michaelbad183531.html, July 24, 2017.
3. Dan Kildee, "The U.S. Can't Afford to Include Japan in the TPP," *The Huffington Post*, November 4, 2012. Accessed at www.huffingtonpost.com/dan-kildee/the-us-cant-afford-to-inc_b_1854359.html, July 24, 2017.

4.  Susan Ariel Aaronson, "What Does TPP Mean for the Open Internet?" Institute for International Economic Policy, George Washington University, November 16, 2015. Accessed at www.gwu.edu/~iiep/events/DigitalTrade2016/TPPPolicyBrief.pdf, July 24, 2017.

5.  Lori Wallach, "Leading Economists Oppose TPP Provision Giving Corporations Upper Hand in Investor-State Disputes," *Democracy Now!* September 8, 2016. Accessed at www.democracynow.org/2016/9/8/leading_economists_oppose_tpp_provision_giving, July 24, 2017.

6.  Aaronson, "Digital Trade Rules and Digital Protectionism."

7.  Wallach, "Leading Economists Oppose TPP Provision."

8.  Aaronson, "Digital Trade Rules and Digital Protectionism."

9.  Fei Shen and Lokman Tsui, "Public Opinion Toward Internet Freedom in Asia: A Survey of Internet Users from 11 Jurisdictions," Berkman Klein Center for Internet & Society, Harvard University, May 4, 2016. Accessed at https://papers.ssrn.com/sol3/papers.cfm?abstract_id=2773802, July 24, 2017.

10. Ibid.

11. Orlando Crowcroft, "Behind the Great Firewall, China Is Winning Its War Against Internet Freedom," *International Business Times*, May 9, 2016. Accessed at www.ibtimes.co.uk/behind- great-firewall-china-winning-its-war-against-internet-freedom-1558550, July 24, 2017.

## Chapter 3: New Regulations Governing Global Internet Business

1.  See European Commission, "Protection of Personal Data," November 24, 2016. Accessed at http://ec.europa.eu/justice/data-protection, July 27, 2017.

2.  See Government of Canada, "Personal Information Protection and Electronic Documents Act," January 27, 2017. Accessed at http://laws-lois.justice.gc.ca/eng/acts/p-8.6, July 27, 2017.

3.  See European Commission, "Reform of EU Data Protection Rules," January 18, 2016. Accessed at http://ec.europa.eu/justice/data-protection/reform/index_en.htm, July 27, 2017.

4.  See U.S. Department of Homeland Security, "Federal Information Security Modernization Act of 2014," October 3, 2016. Accessed at www.dhs.gov/fisma, July 27, 2017.

5.  See Simon Denyer, "China's Scary Lesson to the World: Censoring the Internet Works," *Washington Post*, May 23, 2016. Accessed at www.washingtonpost.com/world/asia_pacific/chinas-scary-lesson-to-the-world-censoring-the-internet-works/2016/05/23/413afe78-fff3-11e5-8bb1-f124a43f84dc_story.html?utm_term=.46f9b9b9906c, July 27, 2017.

6.  Tony Noblett, "Business of IT: Understanding Regulatory Compliance," *Microsoft: TechNet Magazine* (September 2006). Accessed at https://technet.

microsoft.com/en-us/magazine/11a53f92-2a39-46d7-91df-580ffdf44c41, July 27, 2017.

7. Michael Beckerman, "Statement on Fair Use," *IA News*, August 16, 2016. Accessed at https://internetassociation.org/081616trade, July 27, 2017.

8. Office of the United States Trade Representative, "U.S.-Korea Free Trade Agreement." Accessed February 2017 at https://ustr.gov/trade-agreements/free-trade-agreements/korus-fta, July 27, 2017.

9. Office of the United States Trade Representative, "Fact Sheet: Four Year Snapshot: The U.S.-Korea Free Trade Agreement." Accessed February 2017 at https://ustr.gov/about-us/policy-offices/press-office/fact-sheets/2016/March/Four-Year-Snapshot-KORUS, July 27, 2017.

10. Dereje Yimam and Eduardo B. Fernandez, "A Survey of Compliance Issues in Cloud Computing," *Journal of Internet Services and Applications* 7, no. 5 (May 10, 2016). Accessed at https://jisajournal.springeropen.com/articles/10.1186/s13174-016-0046-8, July 27, 2017.

11. Eric Chabrow, "Small Agencies Improving FISMA Compliance," GovInfoSecurity (July 3, 2014). Accessed at www.govinfosecurity.com/small-agencies-improving-fisma- compliance-a-7016, July 27, 2017.

12. Zach Noble, "FISMA Report Shows Pain, Few Gains," FCW (March 21, 2016). Accessed at https://fcw.com/articles/2016/03/21/fisma-omb-noble.aspx, July 27, 2017.

13. International Organization for Standardization, "ISO/IEC 27000:2016," February 15, 2016. Accessed at www.iso.org/iso/catalogue_detail?csnumber=66435, July 27, 2017.

14. See European Commission, "Reform of EU Data Protection Rules."

15. See European Commission, "Protection of Personal Data."

16. Vikalp Paliwal, "Getting Ready for the European Union's General Data Protection Regulation? Learn, Think and Prepare," *SecurityIntelligence* (August 15, 2016). Accessed at https://securityintelligence.com/getting-ready-for-the-european-unions-general-data-protection-regulation-learn-think-and-prepare, July 27, 2017.

17. Tahl Tyson, Thomas Griebe, and Heather M. Peck, "What Brexit May Mean for U.S. Companies with Overseas Workers," *TLNT* (July 29, 2016). Accessed at www.eremedia.com/tlnt/what-brexit-may-mean-for-u-s-companies-with-overseas-workers, July 27, 2017.

## Chapter 4: Are New Internet Regulations Helping or Hurting Business?

1. Dan Quayle, *BrainyQuote.com*. Accessed at www.brainyquote.com/quotes/quotes/d/danquayle102949.html, July 27, 2017.

2. Russell Simmons, *BrainyQuote.com*. Accessed at www.brainyquote.com/quotes/quotes/r/russellsim550791.html, July 27, 2017.

3. Bill Joy, *AZQuotes.com*. Accessed at www.azquotes.com/quote/1046928, July 27, 2017.

4. Meltzer, *Maximizing the Opportunities of the Internet for International Trade.*

5. Melissa McDonough, "The Difficulties of Litigating Cyber Crime," Law Enforcement Cyber Center, March 30, 2016. Accessed at www.iacpcybercenter.org/the-difficulties-of-litigating-cyber-crime, July 27, 2017.

6. Caitlin Cimpanu, "Military Reform, US Pact Slow Down China's Cyber-Espionage Operations," *Softpedia*, June 21, 2016. Accessed at http://news.softpedia.com/news/military-reform-us-pact-slow-down-china-s-cyber-espionage-operations-505460.shtml#ixzz4P8vHuIaT, July 27, 2017.

7. Kaveh Waddell, "Why Google Quit China — and Why It's Heading Back," *The Atlantic* (January 19, 2016). Accessed at www.theatlantic.com/technology/archive/2016/01/why-google-quit-china-and-why-its-heading-back/424482, July 27, 2017.

8. See APEC, "Member Economies" (2017). Accessed at www.apec.org/about-us/about-apec/member-economies.aspx, July 27, 2017.

9. See APEC, "Electronic Commerce Steering Group" (2017). Accessed at www.apec.org/Home/Groups/Committee-on-Trade-and-Investment/Electronic-Commerce-Steering-Group, July 27, 2017.

10. APEC, "APEC Blueprint for Action on Electronic Commerce" (2017). Accessed at www.apec.org/Meeting-Papers/Leaders-Declarations/1998/1998_aelm/apec_blueprint_for.aspx, July 27, 2017.

11. "A Multi-Speed Europe: EU's New Internet Rules Will Hurt the Continent's Startups," *The Economist*, October 31, 2015. Accessed at www.economist.com/news/business/21677175-eus-new-internet-rules-will-hurt-continents-startups-multi-speed-europe on July 27, 2017.

12. Cecilia Kang, "Court Backs Rules Treating Internet as Utility, not Luxury," *New York Times*, June 14, 2016. Accessed at www.nytimes.com/2016/06/15/technology/net-neutrality-fcc-appeals-court-ruling.html?_r=0, July 27, 2017.

13. Paul Carsten and Michael Martina, "U.S. Says China Internet Censorship a Burden for Businesses," *Reuters*, April 8, 2016. Accessed at www.reuters.com/article/us-usa-china-trade-internet-idUSKCN0X50RD, July 27, 2017.

14. Yimam and Fernandez, "A Survey of Compliance Issues in Cloud Computing."

15. Ieuan Jolly, "Data Protection in United States: Overview," *0*, July 1, 2016. Accessed at http://us.practicallaw.com/6-502-0467, July 27, 2017.

## Chapter 5: The Cost of Protectionism on Global E-Commerce

1. Alexander Burns, "*Politico* Interview: Gov. Huntsman," *Politico*, February 23, 2009. Accessed at www.politico.com/story/2009/02/politico-interview-gov-huntsman-019181, July 27, 2017.

2. A.E. Samaan, *Goodreads.com*. Accessed at www.goodreads.com/quotes/7610534-there-is-no-more-precious-currency-than-the-unfettered-liberty, July 27, 2017.

3. A.E. Samaan, *Goodreads.com*. Accessed at www.goodreads.com/quotes/tag/technological-evolution, July 27, 2017.

4. Patrick Moorhead, "HPE Discover Conference Day One: Top 10 Industry Analyst Takeaways," *Forbes*, June 22, 2016. Accessed at www.forbes.com/sites/patrickmoorhead/2016/06/22/hpe-discover-conference-day-one-top-10-industry-analyst-takeaways/#7ba223ee148a, July 27, 2017.

5. BC Net Staff, "Knowledge Doubling," *Boston Commons High Tech Network*, December 10, 2015. Accessed at www.bostoncommons.net/knowledge-doubling, July 27, 2017.

6. Meltzer, *Maximizing the Opportunities of the Internet for International Trade.*

7. Ryan Lawler, "Airbnb Tops 10 Million Guest Stays Since Launch, Now Has 550,000 Properties Listed Worldwide," *Techcrunch.com*, December 19, 2013. Accessed at https://techcrunch.com/2013/12/19/airbnb-10m, July 27, 2017.

8. Joanna Penn and John Wihbey, "Uber, Airbnb and Consequences of the Sharing Economy: Research Roundup," *Journalist's Resource*, June 3, 2016. Accessed at http://journalistsresource.org/studies/economics/business/airbnb-lyft-uber-bike-share-sharing-economy-research-roundup, July 27, 2017.

9. Richard Parker, "How Austin Beat Uber," *New York Times*, May 12, 2016. Accessed at http://www.nytimes.com/2016/05/12/opinion/how-austin-beat-uber.html, July 27, 2017.

10. Meltzer, *Maximizing the Opportunities of the Internet for International Trade.*

11. Aaronson, "What Does TPP Mean for the Open Internet?"

12. See European Commission, "Commission Updates EU Audiovisual Rules and Presents Targeted Approach to Online Platforms," May 25, 2016. Accessed at http://europa.eu/rapid/press-release_IP-16-1873_en.htm, July 27, 2017.

13. Bahjat El-Darwiche, Mathias Herzog, and Rawia Abdel Samad, "Why Are 4 Billion People Without the Internet?" *strategy + business*, May 31, 2016. Accessed at www.strategy-business.com/article/Why-Are-4-Billion-People-without-the-Internet?gko=cd483, July 27, 2017.

## Chapter 6: Business Abroad in a Changing IT Regulatory Environment

1. A.E. Samaan, *Goodreads.com*. Accessed at www.goodreads.com/quotes/tag/idea-economy, July 27, 2017.

2. Amy Goodman, "Economist Ha-Joon Chang on 'The Myth of Free Trade and the Secret of History of Capitalism,'" *Democracy Now!* March 10, 2009. Accessed at www.democracynow.org/2009/3/10/economist_ha_joon_chang_on_the, July 27, 2017.

3. John Cage, "Language and Technology." In Natalie Crohn Schmitt, *Actors and*

*Onlookers: Theater and Twentieth-Century Scientific Views of Nature* (Evanston, IL: Northwestern University Press, 1990), 18.

4. Dani Rodrik, "Put Globalization to Work for Democracies," *New York Times*, September 17, 2016. Accessed at www.nytimes.com/2016/09/18/opinion/sunday/put-globalization-to- work-for-democracies.html, July 27, 2017.

5. Shannon K. O'Neil, "This Week in Markets and Democracy: Protectionism Rises, Mexico Anticorruption Bill Delayed, How Corruption Affects Business," *Council on Foreign Relations*, May 6, 2016. Accessed at http://blogs.cfr.org/development-channel/2016/05/06/this-week-in-markets-and-democracy-protectionism-rises-mexico-anticorruption-bill-delayed-how-corruption-affects-business, July 27, 2017.

6. Alain de Benoist, "Free Trade and Protectionism," *AltRight.com*, July 7, 2016. Accessed at www.righton.net/2016/07/07/free-trade-and-protectionism, July 27, 2017.

7. Elena Holodny, "One of the Central Topics of Donald Trump's Campaign Is a Terrible Idea," *Business Insider.com*, May 14, 2016. Accessed at www.businessinsider.com/protectionism-near-term-economic-problems-2016-5, July 27, 2017.

8. Waddell, "Why Google Quit China — and Why It's Heading Back."

9. *Financial Sense.com*, "Apple Runs Afoul of China's Changing Internet," April 26, 2016. Accessed at www.financialsense.com/contributors/global-risk-insights/apple-runs-afoul-china-s-changing-internet, July 27, 2017.

10. Sanja Kelly et al., "Privatizing Censorship, Eroding Privacy," *Freedom House* (2015). Accessed at https://freedomhouse.org/report/freedom-net-2015/freedom-net-2015-privatizing-censorship-eroding-privacy, July 27, 2017.

11. Ibid.

12. *Financial Sense.com*, "Apple Runs Afoul of China's Changing Internet."

13. Françoise Gilbert, "10 Privacy and Data Security Mistakes Start-Ups Should Avoid," *GreenbergTraurig*, December 21, 2015. Accessed at www.gtlaw-emergingtechnologyviews.com/2015/12/10-privacy-and-data-security-mistakes-start-ups-should-avoid, July 27, 2017.

14. Thomas Zhang, "Common Internet Challenges in China: An Overview," *China Briefing*, issue 159 (October 2015, special edition). Accessed at www.aiia.com.au/documents/event-presentations/2015/national/internet-challenges-solutions-when-doing-business-in-china.pdf, July 27, 2017.

15. Laurie Burkitt, "American Companies Say Doing Business in China Is Getting Tougher," *Wall Street Journal*, January 19, 2016. Accessed at www.wsj.com/articles/american-companies-say-doing-business-in-china-is-getting-tougher-1453260461, July 27, 2017.

16. Zhang, "Common Internet Challenges in China."

17. *Financial Sense.com*, "Apple Runs Afoul of China's Changing Internet."

18. Russ Banham, "The Risks and Opportunities of Doing Business in the Middle East," *Risk Management*, March 1, 2016. Accessed at www.rmmagazine. com/2016/03/01/the-risks-and-opportunities-of-doing-business-in-the-middle-east, July 27, 2017.

19. Ibid.

20. O'Neil, "This Week in Markets and Democracy."

21. Jolly, "Data Protection in United States: Overview."

## Chapter 7: Third-Party Versus In-House IT Compliance Management

1. U.S. Congressman Tom Graves, House of Representatives, House Amendment 95, 112th Congress, February 17, 2011. Accessed at www.congress.gov/ amendment/112th-congress/house-amendment/95/text, July 27, 2017.

2. Simon Mainwaring, *We First: How Brands and Consumers Use Social Media to Build a Better World* (New York: Palgrave Macmillan, 2011), 126.

3. Ed Scannell, "Interview: Symantec's John W. Thompson Talks About Big Picture Security," *InfoWorld.com*, June 16, 2004. Accessed at www.infoworld. com/article/2667741/security/interview--symantec-s-john-thompson-talks-about-big-picture-security.html, July 27, 2017.

4. Yimam and Fernandez, "A Survey of Compliance Issues in Cloud Computing."

5. Ibid.

6. Ibid.

7. See Thomson Reuters, "Top 5 Compliance Trends Around the Globe in 2016." Accessed at https://risk.thomsonreuters.com/content/dam/openweb/ documents/pdf/risk/infographic/top-5-compliance-trends-around-globe-2016-infographic.pdf, August 7, 2017.

8. See Organisation for Economic Co-operation and Development, *OECD Anti-Bribery Ministerial Meeting Programme*, March 16, 2016. Accessed at www. oecd.org/daf/anti-bribery/Anti-Bribery-Ministerial-2016-agenda.pdf, July 27, 2017.

## Chapter 8: Meeting IT Regulatory Obligations

1. John Woolley and Gerhard Peters, President Franklin D. Roosevelt's First Inaugural Address, March 4, 1933, *The American Presidency Project*. Accessed at www.presidency.ucsb.edu/ws/?pid=14473, July 27, 2017.

2. U.S. Congressman Jeff Duncan, "Congressman Duncan Introduces Legislation to End Harassing Census Surveys," Press Release, May 2, 2013. Accessed at https://jeffduncan.house.gov/press-release/congressman-duncan-introduces-legislation-end-harassing-census-surveys, July 27, 2017.

3. Dean Takahashi, "Tim O'Reilly Wants Tech Heroes to Change Government (Interview)," *VentureBeat*, June 24, 2014. Accessed at http://venturebeat.

com/2014/06/24/tim-oreilly-wants-tech-heroes-to-change-government-interview, July 27, 2017.

4.  Yimam and Fernandez, "A Survey of Compliance Issues in Cloud Computing."

5.  John Nugent, "Cyber Security Trends to Watch: 2016," *Forbes*, March 8, 2016. Accessed at www.forbes.com/sites/riskmap/2016/03/08/cyber-security-trends-to-watch-2016/#2319079c1a36, July 27, 2017.

6.  Editors at Cybersecurity Ventures, "Cybersecurity Market Report," *Cybersecurity Ventures* (2017). Accessed at http://cybersecurityventures.com/cybersecurity-market-report, July 27, 2017.

7.  Steve Morgan, "Cybersecurity Spending Outlook: $1 Trillion from 2017 to 2021," *CSO Online*, June 15, 2016. Accessed at www.csoonline.com/article/3083798/security/cybersecurity-spending-outlook-1-trillion-from-2017-to-2021.html, July 27, 2017.

8.  NBC4 Staff, "Chinese Malware Reportedly Infects More Than 10 Million Android Devices," *NBC4i.com*, July 5, 2016. Accessed at http://nbc4i.com/2016/07/05/chinese-malware-reportedly-infects-more-than-10-million-android-devices, July 27, 2017.

9.  Kyle Wansink and Paul Budde, "Global Telecoms Trends for 2017 — Fibre Networks, LTE, 5G, Video Streaming, Smart Nations," *Budde.com*, July 2016. Accessed at www.budde.com.au/Research/Global-Telecoms-Trends-for-2017-Fibre-Networks-LTE-5G-Video-Streaming-Smart-Nations, July 27, 2017.

10. Derek Major, "How Nations Can Ensure IoT Success," *GCN.com*, December 18, 2015. Accessed at https://gcn.com/articles/2015/12/18/iot-national-strategies.aspx?admgarea=TC_BigData, July 27, 2017.

11. Bloomberg Law, "BNA Insights: Distributed Ledger Technology Faces Challenge of Global Standards," *Bloomberg BNA*, June 21, 2016. Accessed at www.bna.com/bna-insights-distributed-n57982074510, July 27, 2017.

12. Lael Brainard, "The Use of Distributed Ledger Technologies in Payment, Clearing, and Settlement," *Board of Governors of the Federal Reserve System*, April 14, 2016. Accessed at www.federalreserve.gov/newsevents/speech/brainard20160414a.htm, July 27, 2017.

## Chapter 9: Is a Uniform Global IT Strategy Possible?

1.  Alex Morritt, *Goodreads.com*. Accessed at www.goodreads.com/quotes/7307855-every-giant-leap-for-mankind-resulting-from-a-technological-advance, July 27, 2017.

2.  Deepak Chopra, "Why Globalism Is a Victory for You," *DeepakChopra.com*, June 16, 2012. Accessed at www.deepakchopra.com/blog/article/3832, July 27, 2017.

3.  Ian Bremmer, "President Trump Enters the Geopolitical Recession," *LinkedIn.com*, November 9, 2016. Accessed at www.linkedin.com/pulse/

president-trump-enters-geopolitical-recession-ian-bremmer?trk=eml-b2_
content_ecosystem_digest-hero-22-null&midToken=AQGz0wprvBw1nQ&fro
mEmail=fromEmail&ut=3IsOKLEwuH4Tw1, July 27, 2017.

4.  Helena Smith, "Obama Calls for 'Course Correction' to Share Spoils of
    Globalisation," *The Guardian*, November 17, 2016. Accessed at www.
    theguardian.com/us-news/2016/nov/16/obama-calls-for-course-correction-to-
    share-spoils-of-globalisation, July 27, 2017.

5.  Meltzer, *Maximizing the Opportunities of the Internet for International Trade*.

6.  Evgeny Morozov, *BrainyQuote.com*. Accessed at www.brainyquote.com/quotes/
    quotes/e/evgenymoro554998.html, July 27, 2017.

7.  Nina Easton, "Your Company Is Probably Going to Get Hacked: Here's
    How to Protect It," *Fortune*, October 24, 2014. Accessed at http://fortune.
    com/2014/10/24/hack-protection, July 27, 2017.

8.  James B. Comey, "Threats to the Homeland," *FBI.gov*, October 8, 2015.
    Accessed at www.fbi.gov/news/testimony/threats-to-the-homeland, July 27,
    2017.

9.  PricewaterhouseCoopers, "Managing Cyber Risks in an Interconnected World:
    Key Findings from The Global State of Information Security Survey 2015,"
    September 30, 2014. Accessed at www.pwc.com/gx/en/consulting-services/
    information-security-survey/assets/the-global-state-of-information-security-
    survey-2015.pdf, July 27, 2017.

10. Rodrik, "Put Globalization to Work for Democracies."

11. *New York Times* Staff, "Across the World, Shock and Uncertainty at Trump's
    Victory," *New York Times*, November 9, 2016. Accessed at www.nytimes.
    com/2016/11/09/world/europe/global-reaction-us-presidential-election-
    donald-trump.html?_r=0, July 27, 2017.

# Glossary

**ACLU**: American Civil Liberties Union
**APEC**: Asia-Pacific Economic Cooperation
**ATM**: Automatic Teller Machine

**BCR**: Binding Corporate Rule
**BRIC**: Brazil, Russia, India and China
**BSA**: Bank Secrecy Act

**CASL**: Canadian Anti-Spam Legislation
**CBPR**: Cross Border Privacy Rules
**CEO**: Chief Executive Officer
**CFO**: Chief Financial Officer
**CFTC**: Commodity Futures Trading Commission
**CIO**: Chief Information Officer
**CISP**: Cardholder Information Security Program
**COBIT**: Control Objectives for Information and Related Technologies
**CRO**: Civil Rights Office
**CTR**: Currency Transaction Report

**DLT**: Distributed Ledger Technology
**DoS**: Denial of Service

**ECSG**: Electronic Commerce Steering Group (APEC)
**EIN**: Employee Identification Number
**ePHI**: Electronic Protected Health Information
**EUDPD**: European Union Data Protection Directive

**FBI**: Federal Bureau of Investigation
**FCC**: Federal Communications Commission
**FCPA**: Foreign Corrupt Practices Act
**FDA**: Food and Drug Administration
**FFIEC**: Federal Financial Institutions Examination Council
**FINCEN**: Financial Crimes Enforcement Network
**FISMA**: Federal Information Security Modernization Act

**FTA**: Free Trade Agreement
**FTC**: Federal Trade Commission

**GATT**: General Agreement on Tariffs and Trade
**GDP**: Gross Domestic Product
**GDPR**: General Data Protection Regulation
**GLBA**: Gramm-Leach-Bliley Act

**HHS**: Health and Human Services
**HIPAA**: Health Insurance Portability and Accountability Act

**ICCMCS**: International Convergence of Capital Measurement and Capital Standards (Basel II)
**ICTSD**: International Center for Trade and Sustainable Development
**IDC**: International Data Corporation
**IOSC**: International Organization of Securities Commissions
**IP**: Intellectual Property
**IRS**: Internal Revenue Service
**ISO**: International Organization for Standardization
**IT**: Information Technology
**IoT**: Internet of Things
**IXP**: Internet Exchange Point

**KORUS FTA**: United States–Korea Free Trade Agreement

**M2M**: Machine-to-Machine
**MENA**: Middle East and North Africa

**NAFTA**: North American Free Trade Agreement
**NGO**: Non-Governmental Organization
**NSA**: National Security Agency

**OECD**: Organization for Economic Co-operation and Development
**OMB**: Office of Management and Budget

**PCAOB**: Public Company Accounting Oversight Board
**PCI DSS**: Payment Card Industry Data Security Standard
**PFMI**: Principles for Financial Market Infrastructure
**PHI**: Protected Health Information
**PII**: Personally Identifiable Information
**PIPEDA**: Personal Information Protection and Electronic Documents Act
**POS**: Point-of-Sale
**P2P**: Peer-to-Peer

**RA**: Reference Architecture

**RAMP**: Risk and Authorization Management Program
**RIFD**: Radio-Frequency Identification

**SAR**: Suspicious Activity Report
**SEC**: Securities and Exchange Commission
**SME**: Small and Medium-Sized Enterprises
**SOX**: Sarbanes-Oxley Act

**TPP**: Trans-Pacific Partnership
**2FA**: Two-Factor Authentication

**VoIP**: Voice over Internet Protocol

**WTO**: World Trade Organization

# Acknowledgments

MUCH APPRECIATION AND GRATITUDE is owed to my wife for supporting me through my many endeavors, including this book. She has only known me while I was employed in the field of information technology, so she has been accustomed to my late-night work without prior notice. Finding time to write, research, and review ideas was a challenge that she made easier for me to accomplish with her encouragement, love, and support.

I wish to express my thanks to all of the writing consultants whose work has contributed to the writing and inspiration for this book, as well as to the researchers, editor, and designer. Without this team it truly would have never been completed.

Malika Dickerson labored intensely through surveys, legislation, and publications to find the facts included herein. Her scholarly viewpoints and intellect contributed much to the development of my opinions regarding the politics of regulatory compliance legislation.

Michael Carroll provided his editing services to the book. His perseverance through personal setbacks and his dedication to his craft is truly remarkable. I am grateful for his professionalism throughout the process.

I would also like to thank my employers and colleagues who have bestowed upon me the responsibility of IT governance. Governance and regulatory compliance is a team effort. I am grateful for your support while we figured out how to most effectively support the needs of the business while meeting our compliance requirements.

# Index

Control Objectives for Information and
   Related Technologies (COBIT), 83
copyright
   fair use, 17, 27, 48–49
   infringement, 16, 26–27, 48
   laws, 27
   protections, 15, 60
   public domain, 17
   regulations, 9, 15–17
Cross Border Privacy Rules (CBPR), 48
currency, 54, 68, 102
   currency transaction report (CTR), 32
cyberattacks, 1, 41–46, 74–75, 90, 97–99,
   107–10
cybercrime, 41–46, 94–99, 107–10
   China, 42, 43
   Sony, 42
cybersecurity, 1, 15, 17, 23, 33, 97, 107,
   110

data
   big, 6–7
   breach, 4, 9, 18, 35, 49, 83, 94, 97–99
   collection, 1, 36, 44–46, 59, 82–88,
      91–92, 97
   encryption, 23, 38, 46, 91, 93, 94, 96
   fast lanes, 50, 55
   flow, 7, 14, 15, 20, 28, 58–59, 63, 102,
      105, 106, 109
   localization, 11, 19–20, 28, 39, 49,
      52–53, 71, 96–98, 100, 110
   personal, 7, 9, 40, 91
   protection, 26, 36–37, 45, 51–53, 58, 69,
      74
   regulation, 44, 82, 83
   storage, 18, 45, 99
denial of service (DoS), 52
Digital Millennium Copyright Act, 26
disruptive businesses, 56–57, 63–64
distributed ledger technology (DLT), 102,
   105–06
Djibouti, 76
Dow Jones, 77
Duncan, Jeff, 90

Easton, Nina, 107
eBay, 16, 59
Egypt, 76
electronic protected health information
   (ePHI, see also protected health
   information), 31, 92
e-mail, 3, 4, 18, 25, 39, 101
employee identification number (EIN), 31
European Commission, 37, 60

European Economic Area, 37
European Union (EU), 1, 9–10, 19, 21,
   35–37, 48, 50–51, 60, 69, 83, 101, 110,
   112
   "right to be forgotten law," 9, 51, 69
European Union Data Protection
   Directive (EUDPD), 1, 25–26, 35–37,
   48, 60, 94

Facebook, 9, 69, 73, 80
Federal Bureau of Investigation (FBI),
   50, 108
Federal Communications Commission
   (FCC), 50, 100
Federal Financial Institutions
   Examination Council (FFIEC), 30
Federal Information Security
   Modernization Act (FISMA), 1, 26,
   33, 94, 95
Federal Trade Commission (FTC), 34
Financial Crimes Enforcement Network
   (FINCEN), 32
financial reporting, 30, 86, 91
Financial Services Moderation Act (see
   also Gramm-Leach-Bliley Act), 30
fintech, 102
firewalls, 48, 80, 93, 99
   "emotional," 71–72
   Great Firewall (China), 7, 20–21, 26, 68,
      75
5G technology, 100
Flórez, Vladimir, 111
Food and Drug Administration (FDA), 48
Foreign Corrupt Practices Act (FCPA),
   77, 82
4G technology, 100
France, 69, 72
Frankfurt (Germany), 57
fraud, 29, 30, 41, 88, 105
free trade (see also North American Free
   Trade Agreement and United States–
   Korea Free Trade Agreement), 4, 13,
   22, 53–54, 65, 68, 104
   free-trade agreements (FTAs), 10, 13,
      22, 27–28
Freedom House, 69–70, 72–73
Future of Financial Advice (Britain), 83

Gaza/West Bank, 76
General Agreement on Tariffs and Trade
   (GATT), 13
General Data Protection Regulation
   (GDPR), 26, 36–37, 44, 48, 60, 63,
   89, 94

www.ingramcontent.com/pod-product-compliance
Lightning Source LLC
Chambersburg PA
CBHW071209050326
40689CB00011B/2290